孙维炎　主编

对外经贸英语读物丛

国际销售合同

International Sales Contract

诸葛霖
王小山　编　著
夏赛花

对外贸易教育出版社

序　言

我国实行改革开放政策已有十四个年头了。十四年来,我国的经济发展取得了举世瞩目的成就,对外经济贸易事业也有了长足的进步。近一年来,外贸形势又有了可喜的进展,新的外贸体制调动了各方面的积极性,使进出口贸易额都有了较大的增长,吸收外资和对外投资也都呈现出新的好势头。

对外经贸事业能不能持续发展,除了其他种种因素之外,一个重要的条件是有没有足够的称职的人才。这些年来,通过多种渠道,多种形式,培养了大批从事外经贸的各类专业人才,但无论从数量还是质量上看,都还远远不能满足需要,都难以适应客观实际的要求,主要的困难似乎在于这些人才发展不够平衡,不够全面,多数人总是缺胳膊、少腿的。如有的人懂得外贸业务,但不熟悉专门知识,外语也显不足;有的人精通有关的专门知识,也已了解一些外贸业务知识,但外语能力很弱,对外经外贸外语更是生疏;有的人外语不错,但缺乏有关的专门知识,对外贸业务和外经外贸外语一窍不通。总之,各个方面都精通的“全才”真是太少了。这势必严重地影响我国对外经贸业务的发展。面对这样的现实,我们对外经济贸易大学的一些同志看到了自己的责任,一致认为需要做一点工作,来改变这种状况。经过商议,我们决定用比较浅近通俗的英文编写一套外经贸方面的专业丛书,供有一定英语基础的外经外贸工作者和在校的大学生阅读，以扩大他们的外经贸专业知识，提高英语水平。我们希望这套丛书能为促进我国的对外经济贸易事业的发展起到一定的作用。

孙维炎

一九九二年十二月五日

于北京

前　言

国际销售合同又称国际贸易卖买合同。一笔交易，有卖必有买，只是视角不同而已。

在进出口贸易的运作过程中，签订合同是中心环节，十分重要。偶有差错，便会带来经济损失，甚至导致政治损失，不可等闲视之。

外贸工作者首先要懂得外贸合同的有关法律知识，了解买卖双方的权利和义务，才可以在签订和履行合同时，维护自己的合法利益，按照有关法律与贸易对手磋商，进行有理有利有节的交涉，圆满地完成任务。

当今进出口业务大多可用英语进行谈判和协商。可以说英语已成为商业上的国际语言。负责起草合同条款的外销员以及履行合同的外贸业务人员应尽可能地熟读大量实用的外贸合同条款。因为合同语言有的不同于一般的句型结构，又有不少专用词汇。多读多用，熟能生巧，是掌握合同英语的必由之路。

本书收集了很多条款实例，读者可以反复比较许多条款相同，但措辞各异的实例，求得更为清楚的理解。这样做还可以边学业务，边学语言，一举两得。书中实例具有一定的代表性，但使用时必须视需要作必要的变动。

本书每页都配上中文注释，帮助读者理解课文和合同条款，本书可供各大学涉外经贸专业的学生之用，亦可供从事外贸教学和对外业务的人员学习参考之用。

由于编者的业务与英语水平有限，纰缪挂漏，在所难免，尚希广大读者批评指正。

编者

一九九四年五月

INTERNATIONAL SALES CONTRACT
CONTENTS

PART ONE
LEGALITIES OF

Chapter

INTERNATIONAL SALES CONTRACT ………… (1)

1 **The Applicable Laws for International Sales Contract** ………… (4)

Commercial Laws-The UN Convention on Contracts for International Sales of Goods-Scope of the Convention On written contract-Important issues beyond the CISG provisions-The Foreign Economic Contract Law of the People' s Republic of China-On applicable law-Breach and remedies-Settlement of disputes

2 **Basic Concept of International Sales Contract** ………… (17)

Contract-What is a contract-Enforceability-Agreement International Sales Contract-International character Sales contract-Different forms of sales contract in international trade-Contents of sales contract

3 **Formation of Contract** ………… (30)

Offer-Definition of an offer-Validity time of offer-Withdrawal of offer-Revocation of offer-Termination of offer Chinese trading practices-Acceptance-Definition of acceptance-Revision of an offer-Late acceptance-Time of formation of a contract

4 **Performance of Contract** .... (47)
The Responsibilities of the Seller To deliver the goods-To hand over the documents relating to the goods-To transfer the Property to the goods-Responsibilities of the Buyer-To pay the price-To take delivery of the goods

5 **Remedies for Breach of Contract** .... (69)
The Three Remedies-Remedies for Breach of Contract by the Seller-Remedies for seller′s refusal or delay to deliver the goods-Remedies for seller′s delivery of goods which do not conform with the contract-Remedies for Breach of Contract by the Buyer-To require the buyer to perform his obligations-To claim damages-To declare the contract avoided

6 **Export And Import Procedures In China** .... (82)
Export Procedures-Preparing goods as required under the contract-Examining and amending the L/C-Chartering proper means of transportation-Documentation

and getting paid-Import Procedures-To establish an L/C with a bank-To make shipping arrangement-To effect insurance-To pay the price and get the title to the goods-To take delivery of the goods and clear the goods from the Customs

PART TWO

Contents of International Sales contract …… (95)

Chapter

7 **Preamble** ………………………………………… (97)

Opening paragragh-Diversity of wording

8 **Object of Contract** ……………………………… (103)

Commodity description-Quality-Samples-Specifications Flexibility in quality-Major and minor points

9 **Quantity and Packing** …………………………… (114)

Different weight and measure systems-Various kinds of weight-More or less clause-Packing specifications-An important condition

10 **Price** ……………………………………………… (122)

Varieties of export price-How to choose proper trade terms-Varients of CIF terms-Quoting export price-Escalation clause-Commission and discount-Open price Price of a complete plant

11 **Delivery** …………………………………………… (137)

Delivery and shipment-Time of shipment-Time of arrival-Shipping arrangements-Seller′s responsibility Insurance arrangement-Special commodities-Transfer of title-Frozen ports-Destination in a land-locked country Optional destinations

12 **Payment** .... (153)

Banker's credit-Exporter's draft-Kinds of credit-Payment on collection basis-How to protect seller's interest

13 **Inspection** .... (175)

Right of inspection-Independent public surveyor-When and where to make inspection-Inspection clause-Price adjustmant-Inspection and certification-Buyer's acceptance

14 **Erection, Test-run and Operation** .... (197)

Import of complete plant-Test-run and operation

15 **Force Majeure** .... (209)

Definition of Force Majeure-Force Majeure clause

16 **Warranty and Remedy** .... (216)

Warranty clause-How to make remedy-Need for limitations-Resort to litigation-Penalty-Patent right

17 **Arbitration, Taxes and Other Provisions** ...... (235)

Significance of arbitration-Place of arbitration-Be prudent .... (250)

Appendix: Contract

PART ONE

Legalities of International Sales Contract

The sale of goods has long been taking the lion's share[1] in international trade. As the world economy grows, international trade takes on many forms in addition to commodity trade, such as technology transfer,[2] leasing,[3] processing,[4] contracting[5] labour service,[6] etc. The volume of these comparatively[7] new forms of trade has been on the increase especially in recent years. It brings about[8] the diversity[9] of international trade. In spite of this development, the sale of goods or commodity trade remains the most important among all the trade forms. It is not only because commodity trade takes the largest share, and is the most common transaction and most frequently[10] encountered[11] in business, but also because it provides the basis on which the other forms of business transactions have evolved[12]. Therefore it is very important for business executives

---

① 占最大比例 ②技术转让 ③租赁 ④加工 ⑤(工程)承包 ⑥劳务 ⑦相对而言 ⑧(使)产生 ⑨多样化 ⑩频繁的 ⑪遇到 ⑫进化、发展

to have a comprehensive[1] knowledge of the commodity trade and hence[2] sales transactions.

The international sale of goods, as it transcends[3] national boundaries,[4] faces more complicated[5] situations and more difficulties in the application of relevant[6] laws and commercial practices than the domestic[7] sales.

First of all, the two contracting parties (buyer and seller) are in different countries. There are invariably[8] differences or even conflicts[9] between the two systems of law; besides, the transactions are governed by and subject to[10] the foreign trade policies and regulations of the two countries.

Secondly, although the contract for the international sale of goods is signed by the seller and the buyer, the involvement[11] of other parties is inevitable[12] for the performance of the contract such as carriers,[13] insurance underwriters,[14] and banks. Because of the involvement of the parties, the seller or the buyer will have to bear more risk for the transactions. The reason is quite simple . the more parties are involved, the more uncertainty they will encounter.

In international sale of goods, it is the sales contract that binds the parties participating[15] in the particular transaction. The contract specifies the obligations or duties of the seller and

---

① 全面的 ②于是 ③越过 ④国界 ⑤复杂的 ⑥相关的 ⑦国内的 ⑧总是 ⑨冲突 ⑩受…管理,并以…为准 ⑪涉及 ⑫无可避免的 ⑬承运人 ⑭承保人 ⑮参加

the buyer respectively[①] and also remedies for the injured party when the other party fails to perform his obligations. Without establishment[②] of a contract the sales transaction is absolutely[③] impossible. Therefore, the sales contract is apparently[④] the core of a transaction. In essence, whatever form the international sale of goods may take, a transaction consists of[⑤] two basic procedures,[⑥] i. e. the formation and the performance of a contract, and it is through these two phases[⑦] of business procedures that our import and export trade is carried out.

In view of[⑧] the importance of the sales contract in international trade, Part I of this book is intended to give a descriptive account of the fundamentals[⑨] regarding the legalities[⑩] of the international sales contract so that foreign trade workers may acquire some basic and practical knowledge of sales transaction.

---

① 各自 ②建立 ③绝对地 ④明显地 ⑤包括 ⑥程序 ⑦阶段 ⑧鉴于 ⑨基本点 ⑩法律方面的规定,涉及合法性

CHAPTER ONE

The Applicable Laws For International Sales Contract

Commercial Laws

Where do business people find the rules of the game when they enter into an international sales contract? The applicable law[①] comes from three sources.[②] The first lies in the contract itself, which comprises principles and requirements negotiated[③] between the two parties and stated expressly[④] as provisions in the contract, which will be discussed in Parnt II of this book. This agreement, however, is limited in various ways by external[⑤] factors which constitute the other two sources of the applicable law: the domestic law of a country which bears upon the contract, and the principles of international business conduct.

Though domestic laws are very important as a source of the applicable law, an introduction to all domestic laws is impossible in a book such as this, nor is it necessary. Therefore the

① 适用法律 ②来源 ③谈判、商谈 ④明白无误的 ⑤外部的

only relevant domestic law introduced here is the Chinese Foreign Economic Contract Law (FECL)[1]. This is done for the very practical reason that when doing business with foreign countries, the Chinese entrepreneurs[2] must first have an idea of what the Chinese applicable law is like.

Most scholars agree that domestic commercial laws in the contemporary[3] world may be divided into[4] two categories,[5] i. e. the "Common Law System".[6] and the "Civil Law System"[7] The Common Law System has its root in the British Law and is now used virtually[8] in all the present and former[9] members of the British Commonwealth[10] plus the largest trading nation, the United States, and to them the most important law governing sales of goods is the Sale of Goods Act of Britain[11]. However, in this area the United States has developed separately[12] from Britain for the last two hundred years and now has an internal commercial law known as the "Uniform Commercial Code" (UCC).[13] The UCC has become a national commercial law with its enactment[14] by all states except Louisiana.[15] The nations which adopt the Civil Law System are primarily[16] countries of the European continent and most of Latin American countries and some others. Though the origin[17] of the system

---

① 中国涉外经济合同法 ②企业家 ③现代的 ④分为 ⑤类别 ⑥英美法系 ⑦大陆法系 ⑧基本上 ⑨以前的 ⑩英联邦 ⑪英国货物买卖法 ⑫单独地 ⑬(美)统一商法 ⑭(通过立法)制订 ⑮(美)路易斯安娜州 ⑯主要地 ⑰根源

traces back[1] to Roman Law,[2] the Civil Law System is based on two codes: "Code Civil des Francais"[3] of 1804, and the "German Civil Code"[4] of 1896.

The third source of the applicable law comes from some trade usages[5] with wide spread international influence such as "INCOTERMS 1990"[6] by the International Chamber of Commerce,[7] "Uniform Customs and Practice for Documentary Credits"(UCP)[8] and the United Nations Convention on Contracts for. Interational Sale of Goods(CISG),[9] which we simply call the "Convention". The Convention is a very important document[10] governing the international sales contract, and we will give a brief introduction in this chapter and also explanations on its provisions in the following chapters.

Trade usages are customary[11] practices established by businessmen of a certain industry[12] through a long time of business dealings. Though they are not the law that binds[13] all international sales contracts, trade usages may be binding if the parties express such agreement in their sales contract. Moreover, in many countries, the law courts have the authority[14] to explain the stipulations of a contract according to the relevant trade usage, if ambiguities[15] arise in a contract. The Chinese Foreign

---

① 追溯 ②罗马法 ③法国民法典 ④德国民法典 ⑤贸易惯例 ⑥《国际贸易术语解释通则(1990)》 ⑦国际商会 ⑧《跟单信用证统一惯例》 ⑨《联合国国际货物买卖合同公约》 ⑩文件 ⑪习惯的、惯常的 ⑫行业 ⑬约束 ⑭权威 ⑮模棱两可的言辞

Economic Contract Law, for example, precisely states that in case no provision is found in the Chinese Law regarding any issue, international customs may be applied to the contract (Art. 5.). Trade usages have been increasingly important in international sales transactions.

The UN Convention on Contracts for International Sales of Goods

Different countries have their own laws governing the sales. Sometimes big differences can be found among the laws. Consequently conflicts of law are inevitable, which hinder① the smooth development of world trade. In order to solve the problem, the international community has been making constant efforts in developing a uniform set of legal principles governing international sales of goods, and the United Nations Commission on International Trade Law (UNICITRAL)② has taken the lead in this drive③ towards unifomity in international trade law. On the basis of the two conventions discussed at the Hague,④ i. e. Uniform Law on International Sale of Goods⑤ and Uniform Law on the Formation of Contracts for the Sale of Goods,⑥ the UNCITRAL has worked out a new unified international sales law. In 1980 the convention was prepared, and in September 1981, 21 countries signed the agreement. Signing

① 妨碍 ②联合国国际贸易法委员会 ③努力 ④(荷兰)海牙 ⑤《国际货物买卖统一法》 ⑥《国际货物买卖合同成立统一法》

the agreement is only a step leading towards ratification[1] but does not constitute ratification itself. The Chinese Government ratified the Convention on December 11, 1986, and submitted[2] the notice of ratification[3] to the Secretary General[4] of the United Nations. By the end of 1986, the number of countries which ratified the convention exceeded[5] ten. Therefore the Convention became effective[6] on January 1, 1988, and China began to assume[7] the responsibliities to observe[8] the provisions[9] of the Convention as a contracting state.[10] In fact, the Convention unifies a great deal of the existing laws and practices in international trade. It is advisable for business executives to make an in-depth[11] study of this important document.

1. Scope of the Convention

The Convention has become the applicable law for an international sales contract only when the buyer and seller have their places of business in different contracting states, nevertheless the choice of law principle dictates[12] that a contracting state's law is applicable to the transaction, when both the seller and buyer agree upon such a contract stipulation. (Art. 1 of CISG) It is noteworthy that the Chinese government, in ratifying the Convention, made a reservation[13] on the latter half of this provision; China disagrees that the Convention extends[14]

---

① 批准、认可 ②递交 ③批准书 ④秘书长 ⑤超过 ⑥生效 ⑦承担(义务等) ⑧遵守 ⑨(法律、条约、合同的等的)条款 ⑩(条约、公约等的)成员国 ⑪深入的 ⑫命令 ⑬保留(意见) ⑭扩展

its scope[①] of application to non-contracting states,[②] and insists that its application be confined to[③] the trade between contracting states. The practical legal effect of this reservation by our government is that the application of the Convention to contracts, signed between Chinese firms and foreign firms which have their places of business in non-contracting states should be restricted.[④] For example, if a Chinese company signs a sales contract with a U. S. corporation, the Convention will govern the transaction since both China and the U. S. A. are contracting states of the Convention. If, however, a Chinese company signs a sales contract with a Japanese firm, the Convention will not be applicable when the contract does not specify[⑤] a choice of law. Since Japan has not ratified the Convention, the Convention can not be applied to such a contract because of the reservation of our government. What's more, according to the Convention, the choice of law principle may allow the application of the Chinese law (the law of a contracting state), and the Convention is not to be invoked[⑥] for the said contract in this case.

Nevertheless, the Convention may be applicable if the above-mentioned Chinese and Japanese firms reach a consensus[⑦] to specify it as the applicable law in the sales contract. This is known as the doctrine[⑧] of "party's autonomy"[⑨] in in-

---

① 适用范围 ②非成员国 ③限制在…范围内 ④受限制的 ⑤指定 ⑥被援引 ⑦达成一致 ⑧理论 ⑨自主、自治

ternational commercial world which is widely accepted and respected. In the Chinese Foreign Economic Contract Law (FECL), a provision is expressly set out① that parties have the freedom to "choose" laws to settle their disputes② on the contract, and the law can be a national law (such as the Japanese law), or an international convention. Therefore, the CISG can be applicable to sales contracts signed between parties from two non-contracting states if they agree to do so.

2. On Written Contract.

The Convention provides③ that the conclusion of a sales contract need not be evidenced④ by writing, and that it may be proved by any means including witness. ⑤This is another provision on which China made a reservation in ratifying the Convention. The Chinese government insists that the formation, modification⑥ and termination⑦ of a sales contract must be evidenced by writing which includes telegram and telex. ⑧In the Chinese law, oral⑨ contracts are discouraged. ⑩

3. Important Issues beyond⑪ the CISG Provisions

The Convention governs only the formation of the sales contract, and the rights and obligations⑫ of the seller and the buyer arising form such contract (Art 4). Unless otherwise provided⑬ in the Convention, it is not concerned with⑭ the following issues:

---

① 规定 ②争端 ③规定 ④证明 ⑤人证 ⑥修改 ⑦终止 ⑧电传 ⑨口头的 ⑩不鼓励 ⑪在…范围以外 ⑫权利和义务 ⑬如果没有另外规定 ⑭与…无关

1) the validity[①] of the contract or of any of its provisions or of any usage.

2) the effect which the contract may have on the property[②] in the goods sold.

3) the liability of the seller for death or personal injury[③] caused by the goods to any person.

The Foreign Economic Contract Law of The People's Republic of China.

The term "economic contract" is regarded as a Chinese invention, which is analogous[④] to "commercial contract" often used in international business world, but its scope is wider than that of the latter, for it also includes the economic contracts other than the sales contracts of commodity trade between enterprises[⑤] or other economic institutions[⑥] of the People's Republic of China and their foreign counterparts[⑦] or individuals.[⑧]

The Chinese Foreign Economic Contract Law (FECL) enacted on July 1. 1985 is an important law that governs business contracts signed between Chinese and Foreign firms including the sales contracts. The other international contracts it governs are those relating to credit,[⑨] labor service, compensation

---

① 有效期 ②所有权 ③人身伤害 ④类似 ⑤企业 ⑥机构 ⑦相应的对方 ⑧个人 ⑨信用

trade,[1] leasing,[2] etc. However, business dealings of foreign investment in China are not governed and regulated by the FECL. There are a number of special laws and regulations for various economic activities. Although it is relatively short and concise[3] as compared with the commercial statutes[4] of the West, the FECL does contain provisions on choice of law, dispute settlement, the specific contents of contracts, performance, breach[5] and remedies[6].

1. On Applicable Law

The FECL adopts[7] the doctrine of "free choice of law" as a principle of Chinese international private law —[8] a breakthrough[9] in the development of Chinese commercial law. The principle has three implications[10].

1) Parties to a foreign economic contract (including sales) are permitted to choose either the Chinese law or a foreign law as the governing law of the contract. If the parties' choice is the Chinese law, the contract is basically governed by the FECL and the Chinese fundamental law[11] — the General Principles of the Civil Law[12] of 1986 which lays down the general principles for business transaction. Under certain circumtances,[13] reference will be made to some other special laws and regulations to tackle[14] particular problems. In practice, due to the imperfec-

---

① 补偿贸易 ②租赁 ③简炼 ④法令、法规 ⑤违反 ⑥补救 ⑦采用 ⑧国际私法 ⑨突破、飞跃 ⑩含义 ⑪基本法 ⑫民法通则 ⑬在某种情况下 ⑭处理

tion[①] and imprecision[②] of the Chinese contract law system, business people often choose a foreign law as the governing law, e.g. the Sale of Goods Act of Britain.

2) If the parties to the contract have not chosen an applicable law, the law which has the closest connection to the subject matter in the case will be applied. As a rule of thumb[③] in the case of an international sale of goods contract, the law of the place of business of the seller at the time of the conclusion of the contract shall apply. However, if the contract is negotiated and concluded at the place of business of the buyer, or if the contract is concluded with its main terms and conditions set by the buyer, or if the contract expressly provides that the seller shall perform its delivery[④] obligations at the buyer's place of business, then the law of the place of business of the buyer at the time of the conclusion of the contract shall apply instead.

3) In case there is no appropriate stipulation in the Chinese law to solve a certain problem, international customs or trade usages may be applied.

2. Breach and Remedies.

According to the Chinese law, breach of contract occurs when one party to a Contract fails to perform the contract or its performance of the contractual obligations does not conform to[⑤] the agreed[⑥] terms and the principles embodied[⑦] in the FE-

---

① 不足之处 ②不明确 ③作为一条经验,根据过去的经验 ④装运
⑤与…一致 ⑥商定的 ⑦包涵

CL. The FECL does not distinguish① between breach of a warranty② and that of a condition③ as does in the British Law. Nor is there such a provision in FECL as "fundamental breach of contract"④ in the UN Convention. In practice, the disputes are left to the discretion⑤ of judges⑥ or arbitrators⑦ as to which factors or whose faults account for⑧ the damages.

Although many differences exist between the FECL and foreign countries' laws on breach of contract, the provisions on this issue in FECL contain ideas derived from⑨ both the Civil Law System and the Common Law System. For example, the idea of "anticipatory breach⑩ of contract" in Article 17 of the FECL can be found in the two systems, in addition, the provisions in this article are virtually the same as those in Article 71 of the UN Convention.

Remedial measures for breach of foreign economic contracts in the Chinese law are somewhat different from the traditional practice in the Civil Law, but similar to provisions of the Common Law. The FECL provides that if a party fails to perform the contract, the other party is entitled⑪ to claim damages⑫ or demand other reasonable remedial measures.⑬ Here in the FECL, damage compensation is regarded as the major remedial measure, and other reasonable remedial measures as sup-

---

① 区分 ②担保 ③要件 ④根本违反合同 ⑤自行处理 ⑥法官 ⑦仲裁员 ⑧造成 ⑨产生于 ⑩预期违约 ⑪有权利(做某事) ⑫要求损害赔偿 ⑬补救措施

plementary[①] ones. This attitude towards breach of contract is quite different from that of the Civil Law where specific performance[②] being required is taken as the first remedial measure. The problem of breach and remedies will be dealt with in detail in later chapters of the book.

3. Settlement of Disputes.

The FECL stipulates four distinct methods to settle the disputes arising out of foreign economic contracts, i. e. consultation,[③] mediation[④] by a third party, arbitration[⑤] and litigation[⑥]. The first two methods are representative of the Chinese character. Because of their culture the Chinese people tend to avoid confrontation and disputation and they usually try to settle disputes by means of consultation or mediation by a third party, in order to reach an amicable[⑦] agreement.

If disputes can't be solved through consultation or mediation by a third party, or the parties to a foreign economic contract do not want to negotiate or to have the case mediated by a third party, the other methods, i. e. arbitration or litigation may be sought after[⑧]. The FECL provides that if the parties agree to settle their disputes by means of arbitration, the award[⑨] of the arbitration is binding and final, and neither party may appeal to[⑩] a court or any other institute for a review[⑪] of the award. In signing an international business contract, the

---

① 补充的 ②实行、履行 ③协商 ④调解 ⑤仲裁 ⑥诉讼 ⑦友好的 ⑧寻求 ⑨裁决(结果) ⑩提出起诉 ⑪重审

Chinese are inclined to stipulate that the arbitration, if any, be handled by the China International Economic and Trade Arbitration Commission (CIETAC)① in Beijing.

In conclusion, as the system of Chinese contract law is newly established and not yet mature, the FECL still has a few shortcomings. A prominent one is that it covers various types of foreign economic contracts, which is likely to result in over generalization② and lack of the relevant provisions in the law which are deemed helpful to identify③ responsibilities of the respective parties. Moreover it is difficult to interpret certain provisions in FECL due to their imprecision. Nevertheless, the Chinese endeavour④ to apply as far as possible the international usual practices to get round the shortcomings so as to ensure smooth progress of economic exchanges between Chinese and foreign enterprises.

---

① 中国国际经济贸易仲裁委员会 ②过于笼统的结论 ③使明确、弄清 ④努力

CHAPTER TWO

Basic Concept of International Sales Contract

An international sales contract is first and foremost[①] a contract. In spite of its special characteristics, it bears the common features[②] shared by all contracts. Therefore, before we delve into[③] the main topic of international sales contract, we might as well study what a contract is. For this reason, this chapter is intended to give a brief account of the essentials[④] of a contract, and then concentrate on the major aspects of the international sales contract in the next section.

Contract

1. What is a contract?

A contract is "an agreement which is either enforced[⑤] by law or recognized[⑥] by law as affecting[⑦] the legal rights or duties of the parties"(An Outline of the Law of Contract). From

---

① 首先 ②共同点 ③探究、钻研 ④要素 ⑤执行、强制 ⑥认为 ⑦影响

the definition, we may find two essential features of a contract. The first is that a contract must be enforceable by law, often referred to as[①] the enforceability[②] of contract; the second is that there must be an agreement existing in a contract. Therefore, in simple terms we may say that a contract is a legally enforceable agreement.

2. Enforceability

The feature of enforceabilety draws a firm line between contracts and social engagements[③] which exist outside the framework[④] of the law, and are binding only in the sense of[⑤] moral obligation.[⑥] When a contract is formed, the parties have to shoulder the responsibility of carrying it out, or suffer the consequences of failing to do so, since the contract is enforced by the law. But what does it really mean by saying a contract should be "legally enforceable?"

The meaning embraces[⑦] the following aspects:

1) There must be mutual promise made by the contracting parties.

A contract must be bilateral[⑧], that is, each party will both make and receive a promise, and the contractual obligations will be binding on both parties, not one of them. This mutual promise is known as the "consideration"[⑨] in the law. The basic feature of the doctrine of consideration is the idea of reciproci-

---

① 被称为 ②强制性 ③约定 ④框架 ⑤在意义上 ⑥道德规范 ⑦包括 ⑧双方的 ⑨(法律用语)对价

ty.[1] That is to say "something of value in the eye of law" must be given for promises in order to make it enforceable as a contract. It goes without saying[2] that in contract for the sale of goods, the consideration for the buyer's promise to pay, is the seller's promise to deliver the goods, or their actual delivery.

2) The parties must have legal capacity[3] or competence in signing a contract.

A contract is enforceable only when the parties put their signatures on the contract. If the contract is signed with an individual, the so-called "natural person"[4] in law, he must be a citizen.

It is universally known that contracts with children or mentally ill[5] persons are generally not enforceable simply because they do not possess the competence in themselves of signing the contracts. If the contract is signed with a company, the person who signs the contract must be the "legal person"[6] of the company, or one that has the authority necessary to make the contract bind the company. On international level, the problem of "capacity of signing the contract" seems more complicated. In China, only those companies that have the govemment's authorization can engage[7] in international trade, and therefore, only these companies have the necessary power to sign enforceable contracts. There are similar regulations on foreign trade

---

① 相互性 ②不用说 ③法律能力 ④自然人 ⑤精神失常 ⑥法人 ⑦从事

management[①] in some other countries as well.

3)The subject matter[②] of the contract must be legal.

The prties can make whatever bargains[③] they please as long as those bargains do not involve an unlawful subject matter, which runs into government prohibition[④] or is against the public policies[⑤] of the country. For example, the selling of drug[⑤] is such illegal[⑥] transaction.

3. Agreement

Agreement is another essential feature of contract. In order to enter into a contract, the parties must reach a consensus on the terms[⑦] provided in the contract; in other words, no contract is formed unless the parties have agreed. Therefore , agreement is the foundation of a contract. When the parties sign a contract, their agreement is embodied within the contract. But sometimes the agreement is witnessed by a written document in which some general principles are laid out in preparation for the signing of a formal contract. In this case, the purpose of the written agreement is to show the parties' intention of entering into a contract, but this is not identical[⑧] with the contract itself.

Generally speaking, the parties are free to make agreement on anything as long as it is not achieved through illegal means, nor is it against the law. This is known as the "parties' auto-

---

① 管理 ①(合同的)标的物 ②讨价还价 ③禁令 ④公共政策 ⑤毒品 ⑥非法的 ⑦条款 ⑧相同的

nomy"[1] principle in law, which means that the parties may independently decide, among other things,[2] the subject matter, the price, their respective responsibilities, dispute settlement and applicable law etc. Nevertheless, the agreement which a contract is based on is subject to a number of qualifications[3].

The first of these is that the law generally applies[4] an objective test of agreement. The law only regards agreement as formed by a coincidence[5] of objectively ascertained[6] intentions. Whatever subjective intentions they have in mind is irrelevant to the contract.

The second qualification is that, even where agreement determines[7] the existence of a contract, it does not necessarily determine all provisions of the contracts or scope of a contract. In other words , terms expressly stipulated in agreement may not by the only obligations binding on the parties. There may be an operative trade or business usage or custom that may be applied to govern the relationship of the parties.

International Sales Contract

As the general characteristics of contract have been made clear in the previous section, the explanation of this particular contract--international sales contract becomes much easier. It is

---

① 当事人的自主权 ②其中 ③资格 ④采用 ⑤巧合 ⑥已确定的 ⑦决定

obvious that the meaning of an intemational sales contract is two-fold; [1]one is its internal feature that it is a contract of sale of goods, and the other is a relatively external one--the international character. We are going to look at the external feature first, and the internal one--the sales contract next, and then to explain some other aspects concerning the international sales contract.

1. International character

What does it mean when we say a sales contract is international? There may be several criteria[2] to determine the international character of a contract i. e.

1) whether the parties to the contract are of different nationalities,[3]

2) whether foreign factors are involved in the business transaction, for example, the goods are in a foreign country.

3) whether the places of business of the parties are in different states.

The United Nations Convention on International Sale of Goods (CISG) describes an international sales contract as a sales contract signed between "parties whose places of business are in different states" (CISG Art1-1) regardless of[4] the parties' nationalities. Apparently the CISG adopts the third criterion. In other words, [5]as long as the transaction transcends

---

① 双重的、两方面的 ②标准(复),单数为 criterion ③国籍 ④无论 ⑤换言之

national boundaries, the contract is regarded as international even if the parties to the contract are of the same nationality. However, the Chinese Foreign Economic Contract Law (FECL) attaches more importance to the nationality of the parties, which means that the first criterion is applied to determine the international character of a contract in the Chinese law. The FECL provides that it applies to[①] contracts signed between a Chinese firm[②] and a foreign one, even if the latter is in China. For it is quite common that in China the idea of internationality is understood as foreign related[③].

Since both the UN Convention and the FECL are very important for our import and export trade, the different criteria for the international character may lead to confusion in its interpretation[④]. Therefore, the combination of the two criteria is rightly used to determine the international character. Thus an international sales contract, in this monograph,[⑤] refers to sales contract signed between a Chinese economic entity[⑥] with a foreign one whose place of business is not in China.

2. Sales Contract

The British Sale of Goods Act (SGA) defines sales contract as a contract by which one party (the seller) transfers[⑦] or agrees to transfer the property[⑧] in goods to the other (the

---

① 适用于 ②公司 ③涉外的 ④解释 ⑤专著、专题论文 ⑥经济实体 ⑦转移 ⑧财产权

buyer)for a money consideration,called price[①](SGA 1-1)

As is know from Chapter l,consideration refers to the fact that contractual liabilites come from both of the two parties. In the case of a sales contract,the seller transfers the property in goods or title[②] of the property to the buyer in a way specified in the sales contract,and the buyer pays an agreed sum of money--the price to the seller so as to take possession of the property. It is based on this reciprocity that a sales contract is formed.

The sales contract is the sale of goods,but not all things bought and sold are regarded as "goods". The SGA provides that goods include all personal chattels[③] other than things in action and money. Things in action may refer to those negotiable instruments[④] like stocks[⑥] or drafts. [⑤] The sale of these things and money are not within the scope of the SGA. The UN Convention 1980 has similar restrictions on the application of the law,perhaps a little more strict. The Convention applies its terms only to the sale of certain goods. Among other things, it does not apply to sales of ships or aircrafts,sales of stocks or negotiable instruments,or sales of goods purchased for personal or household[⑦] use. These exemptions[⑧] suggest that the Convention is a system of commercial rules applicable only between merchants,and is not to be regarded as a kind of international consumer protection statute[⑨].

---

① 价金 ②所有权 ③动产 ④可转让票据 ⑤股票 ⑥汇票 ⑦家庭的 ⑧例外 ⑨消费者保护法

3. Different Forms of Sales Contract in International trade

Since the seller and the buyer are located in different countries, the sales contract between them is, in essense[1], an export contract or import contract for the seller and the buyer respectively. In international trade, an export or import contract may be achieved through various means, the UN Convention 1980 , for example, provides that a contract of sale may be made orally or in written form. However, according to the Chinese Law, only written contracts are accepted, and oral ones are prohibited by the law, and our government has made this stand[2] clear in signing the Convention. Therefore, in the Chinese foreign trade practice, we must always insist on[3] written contracts. In international sales transactions, the parties adopt different forms of written contracts in the light of[4] various situations. Whatever the forms may be, the sales contracts may be classified basically into two major types: the pre-printed forms by one of the parties, and the ones made through bilateral negotiation.

It is quite common that large corporations all have their own preprinted contract forms, which are also known as the standard contracts.[5] Both sellers and buyers may have their standard contracts, on which sellers or buyers stipulate mainly

---

① 实质上 ②立场 ③坚持 ④按照、根据 ⑤标准合同

some commercial terms, or with the addition[1] of some necessary general terms (these terms will be explained later), and then they are countersigned[2] by the other party, the standard contracts will be enforced by law. Standard contracts have their simple forms and complicated forms. The simple forms are often seen as the sales confirmations[3] (printed by the seller), or the purchase orders[4] (printed by the buyer.) which contain generally some major commercial clauses[5]. The application of standard contracts simplifies[6] a lot of paper work in that details which are more or less[7] the same for most contracts of a particular corporation therefore, there need not be specifically typed each time, even if there may be a need for some variable provisions, which can be typed in as required.

Nevertheless, the fact that the standard contract is prepared by one party may lead to some sort of problem, i. e. the party would incorporate[8] terms to his favor[9]. When the other party merely accepts the contract provisions without attempting to negotiate terms more favorable to himself, he would be in a very disadvantaged position in the course of[10] business negotiation or in case of a conflict. The preprinted form contract is, therfore, commonly used only when there is a high degree of trust between buyer and seller, when the amounts in-

---

① 添加 ②会鉴 ③销售确认书 ④订货单 ⑤商业条款,指价格、数量、交货、付款等条款 ⑥简化 ⑦大致、几乎 ⑧结合(意描写进去) ⑨对他有利 ⑩在……过程中

volved are relatively small, or when enough previous business has gone on between them to make repeat orders fairly routine.①

There are times when the parties have to sit together to negotiate contractual terms or conditions in detail. In this case, the long form or detailed contracts are needed. This may happen when the amount of the goods traded is large or the goods are* highly sophisticated machinery② involving a huge sum of money. The completion of sales contract of this kind is much more complicated than the ordinary short form contract. Sometimes the buyer and the seller may hold negotiation for contractual terms for days or even weeks before a mutually agreed agreement can be made. For this reason, the provisions in the contract are discussed more thoroughly, and contain more extensive issues, and thus there is less possibility of disputes arising from the contract. If it has any disadvantage, it is too time-consuming③, which doesn't seem to fit the world's rapidly changing business.

4. Contents of Sales Contract

In convention, a sales contract consists of 3 parts, that is preamble,④ body, and witness clause⑤.

Preamble of contract includes title, contract number, the names and addresses of the parties to the contract, place of

---

① 常规、例行公事 ②非常精密、复杂的机械设备 ③费时间的 ④序言 ⑤结束语

signing, whereas clause,[1] etc.

Witness clause includes date of signing, parties' signatures etc.

Body is the core of a contract which contains basic conditions and general terms and conditions. Basic conditions refer to those commercial terms which determine the rights and obligations of the seller and the buyer. These terms comprise name of commodity, quantity, quality, price, packing, shipment & delivery,[2] insurance, payment, inspection,[3] warranty and remedy,[4] force majeure,[5] arbitration and so on. Basic conditions are the most important part of a contract. General terms and conditions are terms or conditions which are additional to basic conditions or clauses commonly provided in all commercial contracts.

The above clauses are not equally important. According to some law the contractual clauses are classified into conditions and warranties. Conditions refer to those terms involving the nature of a contract. Warranties are terms that act as an assurance[6] by a party on which the other party may rely. In case of a breach, the breach of a condition will lead to more serious consequences than that of a warranty. Generally speaking, if a breach of a condition happens, the injured party[7] is entitled to declare[8] the contract avoided[9] and at the same time claim damages.[10] If it is a breach of a warranty, the injured party can

---

① 结束条款 ②装船和交货 ③检验 ④担保与补救 ⑤不可抗力 ⑥保证 ⑦受害方 ⑧宣布 ⑨无效 ⑩要求损害赔偿

only claim damages. It is noteworthy[1] that the law does not specify what clauses in a contract are conditions, and what are warranties. The common understanding is that clauses on description[2] of goods , quality & specification,[3] price, quantity, delivery time and place, etc are regarded as conditions.

No doubt the parties must perform these terms, no matter what conditions or warranties they are, as they are set out in the contract based on the two parties' agreement. However, the performance of these terms does not necessarily constitute the full performance of the contract. The parties must also perform some obligations imposed[4] by law or some customary practice prevailing[5] in the line of business[6]. For example, the goods provided by the seller must conform to[7] the normal commercial standards, say, rice should be edible[8] for the human beings, though no such provision can be found in the contract. We call those terms expressly stipulated in a contract "express terms"[9], and those not, "implied terms".[10] Once a contract is formed, both express terms and implied terms will become the parties' obligations.

---

① 值得注意的 ②描述(名称) ③规格 ④被强加的 ⑤普遍流行的 ⑥在该行业中 ⑦与……相符 ⑧食用的 ⑨明示条款 ⑩暗示条款(未明确写在合同上的)

CHAPTER THREE

Formation of Contract

A contract results from the agreement between the parties, and the international sales contract is not different. It is formed through actions of offer① and acceptance.② In international trade the offer-acceptance process is not a simple one. When one party (the offeror)③ brings forth④ an offer, the other (the offeree)⑤ may not accept all the terms, and may raise⑥ some different terms. In this case the offeree is said to be making a counter-offer. After repeated negotiation and bargaining--generally by means of telex or fax in modern business--the parties reach a consensus on all the terms and thus the sales contract is formed.

Offer and acceptance are two key⑦ elements in forming a contract. In major trading countries of the world, regulations on

---

① （法律术语）要约，又称发盘，在进出业务中称报盘、报价等 ②接受 ③要约人、发盘人 ④提出 ⑤被要约人、受盘人 ⑥提出（问题、意见等） ⑦关键的

the issue[1] of offer and acceptance may be found in their civil code or contract law. In the Chinese Civil Code and Foreign Economic Contract Law (FECL), there are no provisions on the issue though they do stipulate expressly that the agreement between the parties is the precondition of the formation of a contract[2]. This is one of the issues which need further consideration and improvement. However, as the Chinese government has adopted the UN Convention on Contracts for international Sales of Goods 1980 (CISC), the international sales contracts signed between Chinese and foreign enterprises, where the Convention applies, will be handled[3] according to relevant provisions of the Convention. Therefore, in this chapter an introduction is given to the provisions on the formation of contract and the principles of offer and acceptance in the Convention. Meanwhile we shall study the business practices in China.

Offer

1. Definition of an offer

"A proposal[4] for concluding a contract addressed[5] to one or more specific[6] persons constitutes an offer if it is sufficiently definite and indicates[7] the intention of the offeror to be bound[8] in case of acceptance." (CISG 14-1)

---

① 问题 ②合同成立 ③处理 ④提议 ⑤发给 ⑥特定的 ⑦受约束
⑧表示

From the above definition, an offer is "a proposal for concluding a contract". But not all such proposals will constitute an offer. The proposal, in order to be an offer, must satisfy the following 3 conditions:

1) It must indicate "the intention of the offeror to be bound in case of acceptance".

This requirement① is crucial② for us to distinguish offer from non-offer. The concept "to be bound in case of acceptance" means that once the trade terms raised by the offeror are accepted by the offeree, the sales contract is formed, and the offeror has no other choice but to perform the contract even without his consent③ or confirmation.④

The Convention gives no express provisions on how to judge⑤ whether the offeror has "the intention" to be bound by the offer. In practice, we have to take a close look at the wording⑥ used by the offeror in order to make a correct judgement, to examine whether the offer satisfies the two requirements which will be further explained in the following paragraphs, and whether it contains such qualifying conditions as "subject to our confirmation", which generally is not regarded as an offer, but an "invitation for offer"⑦.

Besides, the judgement may be made according to the ac-

---

① (一项)要求 ②至关重要的 ③同意 ④确认 ⑤判断 ⑥措辞 ⑦要约邀请

tions throughout the process of negotiation, or according to some established trade practices between the parties.

2) It must be addressed to one or more "specific person"

According to the Convention, the proposal for concluding a contract must be addressed to specific companies or persons. It should not be a price list,① or commercial advertisement② distributed③ to the public. Proposals of this kind are also regarded as invitation for offer.

3) The contract must be "sufficiently definite".

This means the terms in the offer must be clear and understood in only one way. The terms must not be vague④ and ambiguous⑤ like "about $1,000 per ton", "reference price⑥ $100 per barrel"⑦ "shipment is estimated⑧ in January". The word "sufficiently" means a proposal must contain enough basic terms to become an offer. The Convention provides that an offer must contain the following three terms: name of commodity, price, and quantity, and it further provides that the fixed price or quantity does not necessarily be the only criterion in determining whether the term of price or quantity is sufficiently definite. "For example, an offer may just set out a method to decide the price not fixing it into a certain figure,⑨ which reflects the fact that prices are changing rapidly on the world

---

① 价目表 ②商业广告 ③散发 ④含糊不清 ⑤模棱两可 ⑥参考价 ⑦桶 ⑧预计 ⑨数字

market, and that parties involved in international sales only set out methods to decide the price in order to avoid the risk of fluctuations①. In fact, some import and export corporations in China have adopted the practice, as is found in contracts signed by these corporations. Price is subject to the average price of the shipping month②. Or * "Price is subject to LMB quotation minus one dollar"③

The provisions on definiteness in the CISG are quite different from the long-established trade practice adopted by Chinese import and export corporations. We must pay close attention to the following two points in signing sales contracts with the business firms in the contracting states of the Convention.

First, the Convention provides that if it contains the three basic trade terms: i. e. name of commodity, price, and quantity, the offer is "sufficiently definite". In Chinese trading practice, we require that an offer at least contains the following terms: name of commodity, quality, quantity, packaging, price, delivery, and payment. Otherwise the offer may not be regarded as a "firm" offer④. Therefore, when an offer containing the abovementioned⑤ three basic terms specified by the Convention is received, we should take it as an offer (if the other two conditions

---

① (市场行情等的)波动 ②"价格定为装船月的市场平均价" ③"价格定为 LMB 报价减 1 美元"LMB(London Metals Bulletin)即《伦敦金属导报》,英国有关金属贸易的定期刊物,每期都发布当月各种金属的国际市场价格。 ④实盘 ⑤上述

are also satisfied), as it has met the requirements of a "firm" offer.

Secondly, though a proposal containing the three basic terms for concluding a contract may constitute an offer, people will find it difficult to do business on the basis of the three terms with the absence[1] of some other important terms. Even if we may trun to other relevant provisions in the CISG for help to conclude the business, we will find it disappointing, for the relevant provisions are quite often not so precise, or sufficiently in detail. For example, when no provisions on packing mentioned in a contract, the seller will provide general packing;[2] when there is no delivery time, it is understood that delivery should be made in reasonable[3] time. The concept of "reasonable time" or "general packing" is difficult to explain, and thus disputes may arise. In fact, international transactions are rarely concluded based on the three trade terms, we should grasp[4] the meaning of "sufficiently definite", and more importantly we should understand that it is the minimal[5] requirement for an offer, and that the CISG does in no way restrict the addition of some other trade terms to the offer. Therefore, for the sake of safety, one is well-advised[6] to set forth[7] the above-mentioned 7 trade terms in his offer.

---

① 不存在,没有 ②普通包装 ③适当的合理的 ④抓住 ⑤最低的
⑥明智的 ⑦列明

2. Validity time of offer

An offer becomes effective when it reaches the offeree (CISG Art. 15). On this point, the laws in all states share the same view, for an offer is an indication of seller's proposal, and the offeree can only decide whether to accept it or not when he receives it. Therefore, if one party expects or somehow learns that someone is sending him an offer before he really receives it, he sends an "acceptance" to the offeror. In this case, no contract is formed even if the content of the "acceptance" coincides① with the offer he receives later. The "acceptance" is in fact an offer, and therefore, no contract can be formed on this unless the other party confirms the "acceptance".

3. Withdrawal of offer②

The withdrawal of offer means that the offeror, for some reason, withdraws his offer before it reaches the offeree or before it becomes effective. This may happen when the offeror finds that the offer he makes contains some mistake, or that the situation has changed which makes his offer unfavorale to him. The common practice is to make use of a faster means of communication③ to send the message of withdrawal so that it can reach the offeree earlier than the offer does . For example, if one sends out an offer by ordinary mail④, he may withdraw it by air mail⑤ or telegraph, or whatever means faster.

---

① 凑巧相一致 ②要约的撤回 ③联络通讯 ④普通邮件 ⑤航空邮件

The withdrawal of offer no doubt[1] provides the offeror with an opportunity to correct his mistakes and avoid losses. Nowadays an offer is often made by, modern means of communication like telex and fax, which makes the withdrawal of offer almost impossible, for once the offer is sent out, the other party receives it in a few seconds, and unless the offeror cuts short the sending, the offer will become effective at once. Therefore, before making an offer, we should consider it very carefully.

4. Revocation of offer[2]

To revoke[3] an offer means that when the offer has reached the offeree, and it has become effective, the offeror acts to revoke the offer thus to kill its effectiveness.[4] The issue of whether an effective offer may be revoked arouses[5] hot debates[6] among scholars from different law systems. The civil law system provides that an offer is irrevocable[7] within the validity time,[8] or during the time in expectation of a reply, while the common law system provides that an offer may be revoked at any time unless it is accepted. The Convention makes some mediation[9] between the two legal systems of the world which agrees in principle[10] that an offer is revocable before the note of acceptance is dispatched[11] but provides that on the following two occasions, an offer is irrevocable:

---

① 毫无疑问 ②中途切断 ③要约的撤销 ④撤销 有效性 ⑤引起 ⑥激烈争论 ⑦不可撤销的 ⑧有效期 ⑨缓解、调解 ⑩原则上 ⑪发出

1)it indicates, whether by stating a fixed time or otherwise, that it is irrevocable: or

2)if it was reasonable for the offeree to rely on the offer as being irrevocable and the offeree has acted in reliance on① the offer.

Though the Convention is a compromise between the systems, its basic attitude is in favor of the irrevocable principle of the common law, for most offers encountered in interntional trade are those with validity time . With the establishment of the irrevocable principle, the Convention will contribute a great deal to the stability of the offer and increase the business manages' confidene in concluding contracts.

The provision has the following implications:

a. It refers to the time between the offer reaching the offeree(it becomes effective) and the conclusion of a contract.

b. "Until the contract is concluded" means that once the offeree accepts the offer, the offeror is deprived of② the right of revoking his offer.

c. The revocation only applies to some offers, not all of them. The Convention divides offers into revocable and irrevocable ones. Most of the offers sent to foreign corporations from Chinese import and export corporations are irrevocable ones, since they generally contain validity time. The common meth-

---

① 依靠 ②被剥夺了

ods to stipulate the validity time of an offer in the Chinese trade practice[1] are :

1) to stipulate the latest time for acceptance.

e. g *OFFER SUBJECT REPLY HERE TENTH…[2]

*OFFER VALID TILL TENTH OUR TIME…[3]

2) to set out a period of time for acceptance.

e. g. OFFER VALID THREEDAYS…

___OFFER SUBJECT REPLY IN TENDAYS…

5. Termination of offer[4]

An offer ,even if it is irrevocable,is terminated when a rejection[5] reaches the offeror (CISG Art 17).

It is widely accepted that an offer loses its validity[6] at the time of the rejection by the offeree. The provision in the Convention has two aspects: first, even if it is irrevocable, the principle still applies to the offer, however the practice in some other countries is entirely different, when the offer is rejected, the offeree can still accept the offer as long as the validity time has not expired[7]; secondly, termination takes place when the note of rejection reaches the offeror, therefore the offeree still has a chance to cancel[8] the note of rejection.

6. Chinese trading practices

In the Chinese foreign trade practice, offers are classified

---

① 贸易做法 ②发盘限10日前复到有效 ③发盘有效期至10日我方时间 ④要约的中止 ⑤拒绝 ⑥失效 ⑦到期 ⑧取消

into "firm" and "non-firm" offers,[1] which may cause some confusion in the understanding of the terms, and may sometimes lead to embarassing disputes.

There has been no unified and clear explanation of the terms "firm offer" and "non-firm offer", they are used as a kind of business "jargons".[2] Generally speaking, the so-called "firm offer" is analoguos[3] to the concept of offer in the Convention. It meets the three conditions of an offer, i. e. it indicates the offeror's intention to be bound, is addressed to specific persons, and sufficiently definite. However, a "firm offer" sets stricter requirements than the offer as is understood in the Convention. According to FECL an offer must contain at least seven trade terms[4] to become a "firm" one, i. e. name of commodity, quality, quantity, price, packing, delivery, and payment. Right here some practical problems in international transactions arise. Some non-firm offers may be real offer from the point of view of the Convention. If a foreign offeree receives a "non-firm" offer from us, which we intend to be an invitation to offer, but which satisfies the three conditions of an offer in appearance, we will be bound by it, for according to the principle of objective test of a contract, the law does not care about the intention of the offeror, but the existence of the agreement counts. In this case, the deep-rooted[5] understanding of a non-

---

① 虚盘 ②行话、术语 ③类似的 ④贸易术语 ⑤根深蒂固的

firm offer among the Chinese that it does not bind the offeror when it is accepted, may cause trouble to our business. Therefore we had better give up[1] the misleading[2] concepts of "firm" or "non-firm" offer, and should straighten out[3] this erroneous idea and make a study of the Convention.

Acceptance

Acceptance is another important element[4] for the formation of a contract. According to the laws of all states, a contract can only be formed when an offer is accepted.

The provisions on acceptance in the Convention (Art 18-2. 3) include the following aspects:

1. Definition of acceptance

An acceptance is "a statement[5] made by or other conduct of the offeree indicating assent[6] to an offer." (Art. 18-1)

To understand the definition we must study the following 4 points:

First acceptance must be judged by the acts or conduct of the offeree, e. g. silence or inactivity[7] will not be regarded as acceptance.

Secondly, the offeree may accept an offer through a statement or other conduct. In international trade, a written statement is the general practice, but according to the Convention,

---

① 放弃 ②误导的 ③改正 ④组成成份 ⑤声明 ⑥同意 ⑦不采取行动

oral statement is also allowed. It must be pointed out[1] that according to the Chinese FECL and the reservation on written contract declared by the Chinese Government when joining the Convention, an oral statement shall not constitute an effective acceptance unless it is followed by a written document.

The Convention also provides that on some occasions, or, by virtue of[2] the offer or as a result of practices which the parties have established between themselves or usage, the offeree may indicate assent to the offer by performing an act without sending a written acceptance to the offeror. The "act" generally refers to the dispatch of goods identified in the offer, or the payment of the price (including the opening of an L/C). The acceptance through "other conduct" is rarely seen in foreign trade transactions in China and it still leaves room[3] for further investigation[4] and study as to whether some certain practices are in compliance with[5] the Chinese FECL and our reservation on written contract.

Thirdly, acceptance, notice or conduct must be carried out[6] within the time of validity the offeror has fixed, or if no validity fixed, within a reasonable time (Art 18-23). An acceptance becomes effective at the moment the indication of assent reaches the offeror, i.e. at the time when the offeror receives

---

① 指出 ②由于、凭借 ③留有余地 ④调查 ⑤与……一致 ⑥执行

the notice of acceptance or when the act indicating assent is performed by the offeree.

Fourthly, the essence of acceptance is the assent of the offeree. The meaning of assent adopted in the Convention is not that of complete acceptance as is provided in laws of some countries, for example, Britain. Instead it applies a comparatively flexible① principle which allows the offeree to accept the offer with some additional or different terms on condition that they do not" materially② alter③ the terms of the offer" (Art 12-2). In this case, the acceptance is still effective unless the offeror, without undue delay,④ objects⑤ orally to the discrepancy⑥ or dispatches a notice to that effect⑦. The question of conditional acceptance is very complex which we shall make a detailed study in the following section.

2. Revision of an offer

The Convention provides that acceptance is the indication of assent to an offer. Therefore, "an acceptance which contains additions, limitations or other modifications⑧ is a rejection of the offer and constitutes a counter-offer"⑨ (Art. 19-1). This is a basic principle in judging the formation of an acceptance. In other words, if the offeree puts forward some different terms in his statement of acceptance, the offer is , in principle, considered to be rejected.

---

① 灵活的 ②实质地 ③较大改变 ④毫不延迟地 ⑤反对 ⑥差异 ⑦表明那种意思 ⑧修改 ⑨还盘

Nevertheless, it must be pointed out that an acceptance containing some additions or revisions may still be effective, if such additions or revisions do not alter the nature[①] of the offer, and if the offeror does not object to the discrepancy without undue delay, and the terms added or revised[②] in the acceptance will be incorporated in the terms of contract to be formed. The distinction between the provision and the above-mentioned basic principle lies in the question of how to distinguish those additions or revisions which alter the nature of the offer from those which do not. Terms considered to alter the terms of an offer materially are listed in the Convention as those "relating to the price, payment, quality and quantity of the goods, place and time of delivery, extent of one party's liability to the other or the settlement of disputes". The above listed terms involving almost all aspects of a contract. Therefore, what non-material alterationis still remains an unclear concept. It is common practice that the offeree, while accepting the offer , puts forward various additional conditions to it. It is not rare that the offeree sends to the offeror his purchase order on the back of which the terms different from the offer are printed. The differences may be partial or complete, which would create[③] difficulties for us to decide whether they are material alterations or trivial[④] revisions. If the additions or revisions are among the above listed

---

① 本质 ②修改、改动 ③造成 ④细小的、琐碎的

items, of course, they may be regarded as rejection to an offer, or as a counter-offer. But if they are not items[①] on the list, what shall we do? As things are very complicated in real business transactions, no distinct line can be drawn[②] in this respect. Therefore, when we receive an acceptance containing any modification, it is always advisable[③] to give a clear answer of approval or rejection without delay.

3. Late acceptance

An acceptance becomes effective when it reaches the offeror within the validity time fixed by him or within reasonable time, which implies that an acceptance, like an offer, may be withdrawn before it becomes effective.

Late acceptance[④] means that an acceptance reaches the offeror later than the time it should do (either after the validity time or reasonabe time). The Convention mentions two categories of late acceptance:

1) If late acceptance is caused because of the delay of the offeree, the acceptance is void, unless the offeror, without undue delay, sends a notice to the offeree to confirm the effectiveness of the acceptance.

---

① 项目 ②划(界限) ③可取的、适当的 ④迟到的接受

2) If, a late acceptance can be proved to have reached the offeror in due time[1] if its transmission[2] had been normal, the acceptance should be regarded as effective, but the offeror is entitled to object to its effectiveness, thus[3] making the acceptance void.

4. Time of formation of a contract

It is a widely-accepted[4] principle that in international sales the formation of a contract is at the time when an offer is accepted. The Convention sums it up[5] as: "a contract is concluded at the moment when acceptance of an offer becomes effective." This provision is not contradictory[6] to the Chinese FECL.

---

① 在一段(适当的)时间内 ②传送 ③于是 ④广为接受的 ⑤归纳起来 ⑥矛盾的

CHAPTER FOUR

Performance of Contract

After a contract is effectively formed. the next step is to perform it. The performance of the contract, in essence, is that the two parties fulfil[①] their respective responsibilities or obligations as are stipulated in the contract. Sometimes in a contract there may be no provisions on certain responsibilities. In this case the parties may act according to the UN Convention 1980, or relevant international trade customs or usages, and, of course according to the Chinese FECL. If one of the parties does not perform his responsibilities faithfully,[②] and completely, he is regarded as breaching the contract, for which he will be asked by the other party to pay damages or suffer from some other consequences. This chapter will deal with the responsibilities or obligations of the seller and buyer respectively.

The Responsibilities of the Seller

The basic responsibilities of the seller are:

---

① 完成 ②忠实地

1. To deliver the goods.

2. To hand over[①] all shipping documents relating to the goods.

3. To transfer[②] the property in goods as required by the contract(CISG Art. 30)

1. To deliver the goods

To deliver the goods is perhaps the most important duty imposed on the seller. It means that the seller delivers the goods as required under the contract, at the place and time which are agreed upon between the parties at the time of the conclusion of the contract. To put it briefly.[③] the seller must deliver the right goods at the right place and right time by the right mode[④] or modes of transportation

1.1 To deliver the right goods

This responsibility means that the seller must deliver the goods in conformity with[⑤] the contract, and must pay attention to[⑥] the following aspects.

1) The seller must deliver the goods which are of the same quality, quantity, and description as those required by the contract and are contained or packed in the manner required by the contract. These are the most important criteria in judging whether the goods delivered are in conformity with the contract.

---

① 交给 ②转移 ③简单的 ④方式 ⑤与……一致 ⑥注意

2) Except where the parties have agreed otherwise, the goods do not conform with the contract unless they:

a. are fit for the purpose for which goods of the quality description would ordinarily be used. For example, rice should be edible for human beings, or buses can take passengers.

b. are fit for any particular purpose expressly or implicitly made known① to the seller at the time of the conclusion of the contract except where the circumstances show that the buyer didn't rely, or that it was unreasonable② for him to rely on the seller's skill and judgement. The requirement for the goods fit for particular purpose goes on a step further from that for ordinary purpose. For example, a racing car③ or a bit④ that can penetrate⑤ alloy steel,⑥ these are goods for particular purposes, which are different from an ordinary car or bit. However, the seller is not always bound to deliver goods fit for particular purpose. The seller is bound to do so under the following two circumstances: first, the buyer makes it known to the seller expressly or implied at the time of the conclusion of the contract that the goods must be for for some particular purpose; secondly, the buyer must reasonably rely on the seller's capacity⑦ in delivering the goods for such purpose. For example, if the buyer orders the goods according to his choice of trade mark,⑧ or uses the description of goods with hi-tech⑨ specifications, then the

---

① 让人知道 ②不合理的 ③赛车 ④钻头 ⑤穿透 ⑥合金钢 ⑦能力 ⑧商标 ⑨高科技

buyer is relying on his own skill and judgement in purchasing the goods, not relying on[①] those of the seller's. In this case the seller is not bound to deliver the goods for the particular purpoes.

c. The quality of the goods delivered by the seller must be more or less the same as that of the sample[②] provided by the seller himself.

d. The goods are contained or packed in the usual packing manner for such goods or , where there is no such manner, in a manner adequate to preserve[③] and protect the goods.

The above-listed four obligations (a-d) on quality of the goods are the ones that the Convention imposes on the seller, i. e. the obligation the seller must perform where the Convention is applied. Therefore unless the parties have mutually agreed not to apply the Convention, the seller must perform the obligations embodied in the Convention even if the contract does not contain such terms.

1.2 To deliver the goods at the right place

International sales contracts may or may not contain provisions on the place of delivery. If they do contain such provisions, the seller must deliver the goods to the place as required under the contract. It is common practice[④] that the parties specify the place of delivery by adopting certain trade terms. In

---

① 依赖 ②样品 ③保存 ④惯常做法

this case, the seller will deliver the goods at the named[①] port of shipment[②] or port of destination[③] according to different trade terms. For example, if the contract specifies the term "FOB[④] Shanghai," or "CIF[⑤] London, shipment in Shanghai" or "CFR[⑥] New York, Shipment in Shanghai", the place of delivery must be port of shipment (Shanghai) not port of destination (London or New York), though the freight is paid to the two destinations. In other words, the seller's duty of delivery nnder these terms is to deliver the goods at the disposal of[⑦] the first carriers.[⑧] However, if the term is laid down as "Ex Ship[⑨] London," the place of delivery will be the destination port London. In this case, the seller's duty for delivery is not just handing over the goods to the first carrier, but rather placing the goods at the disposal of the buyer on board of[⑩] the ship at the destination port. The International Chamber of Commerce (ICC) suggests that if the parties adopt trade terms such as CIF, FOB, etc the delivery site[⑪] should be decided according to Incoterms 1990, not the Convention. The newly published Incoterms 1990 gives detailed provisions on these trade terms, which, among other things, makes a better classification of the terms than the previous editions[⑫]. Incoterms 1990 is a very important document

---

① 指定的 ②装运港 ③目的港 ④价格术语，Free On Board 的缩略形式，即"装运港船上交货" ⑤全称为 Cost, Insurance & Freight.（成本加保险加运费） ⑥Cost & Freight 的缩略形式（成本加运费） ⑦置于……控制下 ⑧第一承运人 ⑨目的港船上交货 ⑩在甲板上，舱面 ⑪交货地 ⑫版本

embracing international trade usage. Foreign trade workers must fully grasp and should be able to use them in their sales transaction.

Sometimes the parties don't set out provisions on the place of delivery. In this case, the seller must perform his obligation of delivery depending upon different situations:

1) When the contract involves[①] carriage of goods,[②] i. e. the seller must dispatch the goods to the buyer, the duty of the seller is to hand over the goods to the first carrier. In this case, even if two or more carriers are needed to carry the goods to the buyer, the seller may be said to have fulfilled his duty of delivery when he hands over the goods to the first carrier, and the risk of the goods, at the same time, has passed to the buyer when the first carrier acknowledges[③] receipt of[④] the goods.

2) If the sales contract does not require the seller to dispatch the goods to the buyer (no carriage of goods is involved), the seller's duty to deliver the goods is to place the goods at the buyer's disposal at the place where the goods are stored[⑤] or manufactured,[⑥] and where both the seller and buyer know at the time of the conclusion of the contract. The goods may be specified in detail (e. g. a valuable painting by a famous artist), or unidentified one to be drawn from a specific stock (e. g. 10 tons of Grade I Rice to be drawn from a specific barn[⑦]), or to

---

① 牵涉 ②货物运输 ③承认 ④收到 ⑤保管存放 ⑥制造 ⑦粮仓

be manufactured or produced in a certain factory.

3) In cases other than the previous two, the seller must place the goods "at the buyer's disposal where the seller had his place of business at the time of the conclusion of the contract". The concept "at the buyer's disposal" means that the seller must take necessary steps① to enable② the buyer to get the goods, e. g. making the necessary preparation for delivery such as making proper packing, stencilling③ the right shipping marks,④ and notifying⑤ the buyer to get ready to receive the goods upon arrival. If the goods are in the custody of⑥ the warehouse⑦ or the carrier, the handover of the relevant documents of title to the goods (bill of lading⑧ for example) will be considered as the seller having placed the goods at the buyer's disposal.

1.3 To deliver the goods at the right time

The time of delivery is stipulated in the Convention as the following:

1) If a date is fixed or determinable from the contract, the seller must deliver the goods on that date. For example, if the delivery date is fixed on July 1, or is "45 days after the conclusion of the contract", the seller has to deliver the goods on that date.

2) If a period of time is fixed (e. g. from June to July) or determinable⑨ from the contract (e. g. 60 days after sight of

---

① 采取必要措施 ②使能够 ③刷上(印记) ④唛头(装运标记) ⑤通知 ⑥在……保管下 ⑦仓库 ⑧提单 ⑨可决定的

L/C), the seller must deliver the goods at any time within the period unless circumstances indicate that the buyer is to choose a date. For example, if a period fixed by the contract is June to July, the seller can decide to deliver the goods on any date from June 1to July 31.

3) In any other cases, the seller must deliver the goods within a reasonable time after the conclusion of the contract. As for how long the "reasonable time" should be, it should be determined by the specific situation of transactions or the goods themselves.

1.4 To deliver the goods by the right mode of transportation

Where an international sales contract often sets out clear provisions on transportation and insurance, the seller must perform his duty in accordance with the contract. However, when the contract sets out no such terms, the seller may perform his obligation according to Article 33 of the CISG.

1)If the seller, in accordance with the contract or the Convention, hands over the goods to a carrier and if the goods are not clearly identified① to the contract by markings on the goods, by shipping documents② or otherwise, the seller must notify the buyer of the consignment③ clearly specifying the goods. "To identify the goods to the contract" means that the seller in one way or another places the specified goods at the

---

① 标明、认明 ②装运单据 ③(一批)货物

disposal of the buyer. Often the seller takes the following measures to specify the goods:

a. to stencil the name, address of the buyer or the contract number on the packing;

b. to designate[①] the buyer as the consignee[②] on the bill of lading or other shipping documents or notify the buyer when the goods reach the destination. According to the Convention, if the seller does not specify the goods by taking the abovementioned measures, he must notify the buyer of the consignment with detailed descriptions of the goods.

The specification[③] or identification of the goods to the contract is an act of great significance in law. According to the laws of many states, it is a prerequisite[④] for the passing of title and risk of the goods from the seller to the buyer. Before the goods are identified, the title and risk[⑤] of the goods can not pass to the buyer in principle.

2) If the seller is obliged to[⑥] arrange for[⑦] transportation, he must sign the necessary contract of carriage,[⑧] charter[⑨] the proper means of carriage so as to dispatch the goods to the right place. For example, if the contract is concluded on the basis of CIF, CFR or Ex Ship terms, the seller is responsible for shipping arrangements such as chartering vessels[⑩] and booking space.[⑪] If the goods are perishable,[⑫] the seller must check if a

---

① 指明 ②收货人 ③载明、详述 ④先决条件 ⑤风险 ⑥有义务（做某事） ⑦安排 ⑧运输合约 ⑨租 ⑩船只 ⑪订舱 ⑫易腐烂的

vessel with refrigeration facilities[①] is available,[②] while if the contract is concluded on the basis of FOB, the seller generally has no obligation to make shipping arrangements unles the contract otherwise provides. His obligation ends when he delivers the goods to the shipping port and place the goods on board of the ship specified by the buyer.

3) If the seller is not bound to effect insurance in respect of the carriage of the goods, he must, at the buyer's request,[③] provide him with all available information necessary to enable him to effect such insurance. In international trade it is often the trade terms that determine which party arranges insurance. For example, FOB or CFR contracts mean that the seller is not responsible for insurance, while he must do so in the case of a CIF contract. The purpose of the provision in the Convention is that when not responsible for effecting insurance, the seller should provide necessary and timely[④] information to the buyer so that the buyer can make arrangement for insurance.

2. To hand over the documents relating to the goods

In international sales, shipping documents play an importent role, and they are indispensable[⑤] for the buyer to take delivery and resell[⑥] the goods and deal with custom entries[⑦] and other formalities[⑧]. According to international trade conventions, in most cases, the seller is bound to provide the buyer

---

① 冷冻设施 ②能得到的,具备 ③应买方的要求 ④及时的 ⑤不可缺少的 ⑥转售 ⑦进口报关 ⑧手续

with all documents relating to the goods.

The Convention provides that if the seller is bound to hand over documents relating to the goods, he must hand them over at the time and place and in the form required by the contract (Art 34). The documents relating to the goods often include bill of lading, insurance policy, [1] commercial invoice, [2] and sometimes consular invoice, [3] certificate of origin, [4] weight memo[5] etc. The Convention also provides that if the seller has handed over documents before the specified time, he may, up to that time, cure[6] any lack of conformity in the documents, if the exercise[7] of this right does not cause the buyer unreasonable inconvenience[8] or unreasonable expense. However, the buyer retains[9] the right to claim damages as provided in the Convention.

3. To transfer the property in goods

To transfer the property in goods is, in essence, to transfer the ownership of the goods from the seller to the buyer, which is completed by the seller's placing the physical goods at the disposal of the buyer, or his handing over the necessary documents to the buyer representing[10] the title to the goods. The Convention provides that the seller must deliver the goods which are free from any right or claim of a third party, unless the buyer agrees to take the goods subject to that right or claim (Art. 41).

---

① 保险单 ②商业发票 ③领事发票 ④原产地证明书 ⑤重量单 ⑥纠正 ⑦行使(权利率) ⑧不便 ⑨保留 ⑩代表

This is known in the laws of some countries as the warranty for the right of goods delivered by the seller, i. e. the seller must ensure that the buyer possesses[①] the goods lawfully and safely so that he would not be disturbed by any third party. To put it more precisely, if the seller should sell to the buyer goods which he has got through illegal means, he is regarded as violating[②] the obligations of a seller, for once the real owner of the goods exercises the right to recourse[③] by accusing[④] the buyer of illegal possession of the goods, the buyer will run into[⑤] the trouble of litigation, which the buyer detests[⑥]. Whether the buyer, without any idea of the seller's so doing, will be protected by law, remains a question accoridng to the Convention. In Art. 4 the Convention provides that it is not concerned with "the effect which the contract may have on the property in the goods sold". The problem can only be tackled by the civil codes of the countries concerned. The Convention is only concerned with what rights the buyer may have vis-a-vis[⑦] the seller, and what liabilities the seller must assume vis-a-vis the buyer. The purpose of the provision in the Convention is to protect the interest[⑧] of the bona fide[⑨] buyer, for what he buys is the goods, and definitely not a lawsuit.[⑩]

The Convention also provides that the goods delivered by

---

① 拥有 ②违反 ③追索权 ④控告 ⑤陷入 ⑥憎恶、痛恨 ⑦面对面，相对 ⑧利益 ⑨善意的 ⑩法律诉讼

the seller should be free from any right or claim of a third paryt based on industrial property[①] or other intellectual property.[②]

The issue of industrial property or other intellectral property also involves a third party′s right or claim. In international trade, the infringement[③] on industrial property of a certain party, including patent[④] and trade mark,[⑤] often occurs in countries other than that of the seller. Therefore, as far as violation of industrial property is concerned, the seller may not know as much about the situation in other countries as in his own country, besides, quite frequently in international trade the buyer resells the goods he has received to other countries, resulting in violation of the industrial property in the buyer's country, although it may not constitute such a violation in the seller's country. Industrial property partakes[⑥] of regional character,[⑦] as each state grants[⑧] such rights independently[⑨]. On other occasions, violation of industrial property of a third party may take place when the seller processes or manufactures the goods as per the technical drawings,[⑩] designs[⑪] or patterns furnished[⑫] by the buyer. In this case, the liability for tort[⑬] is to be borne by the buyer instead of the seller. In view of these situations, the Convention sets out the following limitations on the liability of the seller to the buyer in relation to the violation of a third party's industrial property.

---

① 工业产权 ②知识产权 ③侵权 ④专利 ⑤商标 ⑥带有(某种性质或特征) ⑦地方特色 ⑧给予 ⑨独立的 ⑩技术图纸 ⑪设计 ⑫提供 ⑬侵权

1) The seller is bound to take the liability of paying damages① to the buyer only when he knew or could not have been unaware of the fact the third party may request the right or claim on the goods based on indutrial property at the time of the conclusion of the contract.

2) The seller is not always held responsible for any right or claim of a third party based on industrial property, the law (of patent or trade mark) of the countries where the goods will be resold or otherwise used will govern. He is held responsible in this respect only under the following circumstances:

a. where it was contemplated② by the parties at the time of conclusion of the contract that the goods would be resold or otherwise used in a certain country. Since the parties (including the seller) have known already that the goods will be resold to that country, the seller must make sure③ that the goods do not violate the industrial property.

b. in any other case under the law of the state where the buyer has his place of business.

3) The duty of the seller relating to the industrial or intellectual property does not extend to cases where

a. at the time of the conclusion of the contract the buyer knew or could not have been unaware of the right or claim.

b. the right or claim results from the seller's technical

---

① 赔偿损失 ②期望、打算 ③确信、保证

drawings, designs, formulas[①] or other such specifications furnished by the buyer.

However, it must be pointed out that the Convention is only concened with obligations of the seller to the buyer, and the relation between the seller and the buyer. while the right of any third party is not governed by the Convention. When a third party finds his industrial or intellcetual property voilated by the seller or the buyer, he is entitled to exercise the right to litigate according to laws of the countries concened. Neither the seller nor the buyer can evade[②] his obligations to the third party by quoting[③] the "non-governing" provision in the Convention.

Responsibilities of the Buyer

The basic responsibilities of the buyer are of two aspects:

1. to pay the price for the goods, and

2. to take delivery of the goods. The buyer must perform the two basic duties pursuant to[④] the relevant provisions under the contract, and if there is no provisions on some aspects, the buyer may perform his duties in accordance with the applicable trade usages, and of coures, the UN Convention 1980

1. To pay the price for the goods

To perform the obligation of paying the price, the buyer

---

① 公式 ②逃脱 ③引用 ④依据

must comply with[1] necessary formalities of payment, and pay the sum of money at the time and the place as required under the contract.

1.1 To comply with necessary formalitis of payment

This duly includes taking such steps or complying with such formalities as may be required under the contract or any law and regulations to enable payment to be made, which means that the buyer must make the necessary preparation so that it will be a part of his duty of payment. The preparation work mainly refers to (a)applying[2] to a bank to open[3] a letter of credit[4] or guarantee or payment[5] required under the contract(b)in countries exercising foreign exchange control,[6]submitting[7] the sales contract to the institutions concerned for approval,[8]so as to get the foreign exchange necessary to pay for the price in compliance with the relevant laws or regulations of the state.

1.2 The place of payment

In international trade, the place of payment is of vital[9] importance for the parties, especially for the buyer. For, if the place of payment is in a state that exercises foreign exchange control or that limits the remittance[10] of foreign exchange out of the state for lack of "hard currency",[11]the buyer cannot per-

---

① 遵照…做 遵照…做 ②申请 ③开具 ④信用证 ⑤付款保证书 ⑥外汇管制 ⑦呈交 ⑧批准 ⑨十分、极为(重要的) ⑩汇出 ⑪硬通货

form his obligation of payment, and the seller cannot get the payment for the goods. Therefore, the parties generally set out provisions on the methods and place of payment so that the buyer can pay the price smoothly.[①] In case, there are provisions specifying the place of payment in the contract, the buyer must strictly follow the provisions. However, if no provision on the place of payment is found in the contract, the buyer must make the payment, according to Convention, at the following places:

1) the seller's business place. If the seller has more than one business places, the buyer should pay the price at the business place* which has the closest relation with the contract and its perfromfance.[②]

2) if the price is to be paid against[③] the handover[④] of the goods or documents representing title to the goods, at the place where the handover takes place.

In international sale, when the price is fixed on the basis of FOB, CFR, or CIF, it is common practice to make payment[⑤] in exchange for the shipping documents, bill of lading for example, the so-called "documents against payment" (D/P) D/P[⑥]. Whether it is documentary collection[⑦] or documentary L/C,[⑧] the seller's handing over of the specified shipping documents is the prerequisite to the payment of the goods. But the point is

---

① 平稳地、顺利地 ②和合同及其履行最相关的 ③以…为交换条件 ④交出 ⑤付款 ⑥付款交单 ⑦跟单托收 ⑧跟单信用证

where the documents should be handed over, should they be handed over at the seller's place of business or the buyer's? Judging from the usual practice, one may feel it safe to say[①] that if the price is paid in the form of documentary collection, the seller should, through the collecting bank,[②] hand over the documents in the country where the buyer's place of business is located; if the payment is made by documentary credit, the seller generally negotiates the letter of credit with the negotiating bank[③] in the exporter's country (Where the seller's place of business is located); after the documents are transmitted[④] to the opening bank,[⑤] it in turn[⑥] notifies the buyer to get them if the letter of credit has named a bank in a third country as the paying bank,[⑦] the seller, of course, must contact the bank in the third country for handing over the documents and get paid from this bank.

1.3 The time of payment

The general principle concerning the time of payment is that the buyer should pay the price at the time when the goods are delivered or the documents of title are handed over, if there is no detailed provision on the time of payment in the contract. If the contract sets out a specific date for the payment of goods, or some arrangement of down payment[⑧] or deferred

---

① 这样说，不会有错 ②托收行，代收行 ③议付行 ④传递 ⑤开证行 ⑥(按某种顺序)接着 ⑦付款行 ⑧预付款

payment[1] by the buyer, the buyer must pay the price as required under the contract, and there is no need for any request or compliance with any formality on the part of[2] the seller.

1.4 Payment and inspection

The buyer is not bound to pay the price until he has an opportunity to examine[3] the goods, unless the procedures for delivery or payment agreed upon by the parties are inconsistent[4] with his having such opportunity (CISG Art. 8). The purpose of the provision is to protect the buyer's interest and enable him to have an opportunity to inspect the goods in case the seller defaults[5] in delivery. However, the buyer may not have proper opportunity to examine the goods before making payment, especially when the sales contract is formed on the basis of CIF, CFR, or FOB, for unless the contract expressly stipulates such provision as "payment after the arrival and examination of the goods", the seller, according to international trade practices, can require the buyer to pay the price after handing over the shipping documents. When the buyer pays the price, the goods may be still on their way, i.e. in transit, and in this case the buyer can only examine the goods after their arrival. This is why the Convention provides that the buyer is not entitled to examine the goods "if procedures for delivery or payment agreed upon by the parties are inconsistent with his hav-

---

① 延期付款 ②在(卖方)…方面 ③检查 ④不符 ⑤欺诈

ing such opportunity". But this does not mean that the buyer is deprived of the right to examine the goods, which may be exercised after the arrival of the goods at destination. If he finds the goods not in conformity with the contract, the buyer is still entitled to claim damages or take other remedial measures. But the buyer must examine the goods* within the shortest possible time,① or he will lose "the right to rely on a lack of conformity of the goods". As for the place of inspection, the Convention mentions two situations: a) if the contract involves carriage of goods (e. g. CIF or FOB contracts), the inspection may be deferred until arrival of the goods at the destination; b) if the goods are redirected② or the buyer has arranged to redispatch③ them, which deprives the buyer of a reasonable opportunity for inspection of the goods, and if at the time of the conclusion of the contract the seller knows or ought to have known of the possibility of such redirection or redispatch, examination may be deferred until after the goods have arrived at the final destination. This provision is of practical significance in our international trade practice. If the imported goods have to be redispatched to an inland④ city where examination is to take place, we should notify the seller to that effect⑤ at the conclusion of the contract. The best choice is to set out in the contract that the goods may be redispatched or transhipped⑥ to some other

---

① 在尽可能短的时间内 ②重新确定(如何办理) ③重新发送(到另外地方) ④内陆 ⑤将这件事的内容(告知) ⑥转运

place, so as to avoid any possible disputes over this issue.

2. To take delivery of the goods①

Another basic obligation of the buyer is to take delivery of the goods, which consists in:

1) Doing all the acts which could reasonably be expected of him in order to enable the seller to make delivery. In FOB contracts, the cooperation② of the buyer is indispensable. Under FOB terms, carriage of the goods is arranged by the buyer. In case the buyer does not send the proper vessel to the port of shipment by the time required in the contract, the seller cannot perform his duty of delivery. In this case, the buyer is considered to have breached the contract

2) Taking over the goods. Sometimes this obligation of the buyer will directly influence③ the seller's interests. If the seller is bound to deliver the goods through carriers (CIF or CFR), he often requires the buyer to unload④ the goods from the carrying vessel and take them over⑤ as soon as possible. When the carriage is based on the arrangement of a charter party, ⑥it often involves payment of demurrage⑦ or despatch money. ⑧ In case the goods arrive at the port of destination, and the buyer does not unload the cargo punctually⑨ and take over the goods in time, the seller must pay the demurrage, unless the contract sets out a clause that the expenses in this connection will be

---

① 提货 ②合作 ③影响 ④卸货 ⑤取走 ⑥租船契约 ⑦滞期费 ⑧速遣费 ⑨按时

paid by the buyer. More important is that, if the buyer fails to take over the goods in time, the damage or loss caused to the goods during the time will be borne[1] by the buyer. For now the seller has placed the goods at the buyer's disposal, and the risk has passed to the buyer, therefore, the buyer must be responsible for the loss of or damage to the goods.

① 承担

CHAPTER FIVE

Remedies For Breach of Contract

The Three Remedies

In most cases, bona fide party to an international sales contract will do his best to perform his duties either as a seller or a buyer, after the conclusion of the contract. However, it is not rare that either party to a contract may fail to perform his duties, or his performance is inconsistent with the terms provided in the contract. The non-performance[1] or breach of the contract may come from either the seller or the buyer. For example, the seller may refuse, or delay the delivery of the goods, or deliver goods not in conformity with the contract; while the buyer may refuse to take delivery of the goods or refuse to make payment etc. In case one party breaches the contract, he may cause damage[2] or loss[3] to the other, who is entitled to take remedial measures according to the contract and the law.

Most international sales contracts contain a claim clause[4] in which the principles, time and applicable law of remedy are

---

① 不履行(合同等) ②损害 ③损失 ④索赔条款

provided. When one party breaches the contract, the other may invoke[①] the relative contract stipulation to file[②] a claim and get proper remedy. When there is no such clause found in the contract, the injured party may resort to[③] the law for remedial measures. In this case, the international private law may be applied, in other words, the law with which the contract has the closest relation will be the applicable law. Provisions on remedy are quite different in the Civil Law System and the Common Law System. The UN Convention 1980 in some way reconciles[④] the differences between the two major legal systems of the world. Most scholars believe that is why the Convention is now applied to a increasing number of international sales contracts. Therefore, let us take a look at the provisions on remedy stipulated in the Convention.

The acts of breach of contract are varied,[⑤] for which the injured party is entitled to claim for different remedies. Generally speaking,[⑥] there are three remedial measures which the injured party may apply* asking for specific performance, claiming damages, and declaring the contract avoided.[⑦] The Convention classifies the breaches of contract into two major categories:* fundamental breach and non-fundamental breach.[⑧] The convention defines fundamental breach as one"results

---

① 援引 ②提出(索赔等) ③求助于，诉诸 ④接合 ⑤各不相同 ⑥一般来说 ⑦要求实际履行，要求损害赔偿，宣布合同无效 ⑧根本违反合同与非根本违反合同

in such detriment[1] to the other party as to substantially deprive him of what he is entitled to expect under the contract"(Art. 25). If the breach of contract is a fundamental one, the injured party may avoid the contract as well as claim for damages; when a non-fundamental breach occurs[2] the injured party can only claim damages and can not declare the contract* null and void[3]. This differentiation between the fundamental and non-fundamental breach is similar to that between breach of condition and that of warranty in the British law. If the breach of contract is regarded as a breach of condition, the injured party may declare the contract null and void and claim damages as is the consequence of a fundamental breach. But these two cases of differentiation are not of the same nature[4]. The British law considers[5] that conditions are of more importance as contractual terms than warranties, and breach of condition may lead to the cancellation[6] of the contract, even if the actual loss or damages incurred[7] is a minor one; while the Convention determines a fundamental breach according to the seriousness of the loss or damage to the injured party, i. e. it is serious enough to "substantially deprive him of what he is entitled to expect under the contract". Obviously, we can see that the Convention adopts a more practical and flexible attitude[8] toward the issue of breach and remedy. There are, practically speaking, three

---

① 损害 ②发生 ③无效 ④性质 ⑤认为 ⑥取消 ⑦造成，招致 ⑧态度

remedies for the breach of contract. First, claiming damages is the basic and most commonly used measure in practice, for the parties to a contract may apply is for any injury[1] resulting from[2] any breach of contract. The Convention provides that the injured party, buyer and seller alike "is not deprived of any right he may have to claim damages by exercising his right to other remedies" (Art. 45-2). Secondly, declaring the contract null and void can only be applied when the breach is a fundamental breach, or a breach of condition. Thirdly, asking for specific performance is a bit more sophisticated, on which the provisions of the Civil Law and Common Law Systems are widely different. Though it is regarded as one of the remedies under the Convention, specific performance is restricted by Article 28 as the following: "a court is not bound to enter into a judgement[3] for specific performance unless the court would do so under its own law". In other words, when the injured party appeals to a court for specific performance according to the Convention, it is up to the court as to whether it will enter into a judgement of that kind, and the law which the judges apply is not the Convention, but the law of the state where the court is located. For example, courts in Civil law countries may give such verdict,[4] while counts in Common Law countries may not do so. The former regard specific performance as the major remedy, the latter regard it as an auxiliary[4] measure. The pro-

---

① 伤害 ①由…而引起 ②(作出)裁决 ③判决 ④辅助的

visions on the issue under the Convention reflect the reconciliation between the two major legal systems.

Remedies for Breach of Contract by the Seller

1. Remedies for Seller's refusal or delay to deliver the goods.

After the conclusion of a sales contract, the seller may delay, even refuse to deliver the goods for various reasons. Sometimes it is because the seller has encountered insurmountable① difficulty in delivering the goods, and he asks permission from the buyer to postpone the delivery for some time, say one month. However, there are times that the seller simply does not want to deliver the goods for drastic change② in prices on the international market; in this case he may refuse to deliver the goods even though the buyer may possibly agree to postponement of delivery. Such delay or refusal of delivery may cause serious damage or loss on the part of the buyer. Then, what measures may he take to remedy the damage or loss? There may be three options③ for the buyer:

1) To require the seller to perform the duty of delivery. This is what people call the remedy of specific performance. The application of this remedy, however, is restricted by Article 28 of the Convention for the reasons as above-stated④. There-

---

① 不可克服的 ②巨大变化 ③选择 ④以上所述

fore, the buyer may not get the verdict enforcing the seller's delivery of the goods as he expects even if he appeals to court for such a verdict. For the court "is not bound" to do so, this remedy is not often used by parties who choose the Convention as the governing law.

2) To declare the contract avoided. The application of this remedial measure is conditional① only when the failure by the seller to perform his obligation "amounts to② a fundamental breach of contract", the buyer can declare the contract avoided. As is known to us that a fundamental breach is a breach of contract that subsbantially depriver the injured party of what he expects from the contract. When non-delivery occurs, the buyer cannot immediately declare the contract avoided after the seller has committed such a breach, for non-delivery or late delivery itself does not amount to a fundamental breach. Therefore, the buyer may allow the seller additional③ time, and if the seller still does not deliver the goods within the additional period of time fixed by the buyer, or he simply declares that he will not deliver within that period, the buyer may declare the contract avoided. Only by this time, does the conduct of the seller constitute a fundamental breach. However, in cases where the seller has delivered the goods during the additional period set by the buyer, the buyer loses his right to declare the contract avoided.

---

① 有条件的 ②达到(…程度)相当于 ③额外的

3)To claim damages. To claim damages is a major remedy for breach of contract. Accoridng to the Convention, the buyer still maintains[1] the right to claim damages even if he has resorted to other remedial measures. But how much should the damages be? The principles for determining the sum[2] of damages are varied in different laws. The Convention provides that damages for breach of contract consist of a sum equal to the loss, including loss of profit[3] suffered by the injured party as a consequence of the breach, and the damages may not exceed the loss which the party in breach foresaw[4] or ought to have foreseen at the time of the conclusion of the contract, in the light of[5] the facts and matters of which he then knew or ought to have known, as a possible consequence of the breach of contract. The basic principle for damages claim is that the damages paid will enable the economic state[6] of the injured party to be recovered[7] to that extent[8] where the contract would have been performed.

In case of non-delivery,[9] the buyer may declare the contract avoided. If, after avoidance of the contract, he has bought goods in replacement[10]. In a reasonable manner and within a reasonable time, the buyer may claim damages to the amount that can recover the difference between the contract price and

---

① 保留 ②钱数 ③利润 ④预见 ⑤依据 ⑥经济状态 ⑦恢复 ⑧程度 ⑨不发货 ⑩作为替代

the price in the substitute[1] transaction as well as other damages caused by the breach or the buyer may not enter into the substitute transaction after he declares the contract avoided; he may claim damages to recover the difference between the contract price and the prevailing[2] price at the place of delivery, as well as other damages caused by the breach.

Two points are worthy of special attention: first, according to the Convention and laws of many states, the buyer must take reasonable measures to prevent further losses, say, buying goods in replacement. If he does not do so, which causes further losses, he is not entitled to claims damages for the further loss which could have been prevented; secondly, when the buyer claims damages, he does not have to prove whether the conduct[3] of the seller contains any fault. If he can show evidences that the seller does not perform the obligations under the contract, which causes damages to him, the buyer may exercise the right to claim damages.

2. Remedies for seller's delivery of the goods which do not conform with the contract.

In performing the contract, the seller sometimes delivers goods which do not conform with the contractual provisions on quality, specification, quantity, packing or design, etc. According to the Convention, when the goods delivered contain defects

---

① 替代 ②现行的 ③行为

not in conformity with these provisions, the buyer may resort to the following remedies.

1) In case of fundamental breach of contract, the buyer may require the delivery of substitute goods, or declare the contract avoided.

The determination of whether the breach is a fundamental one depends on① the extent to which the goods do not conform with the contract. If the inconformity② is serious enough as to substantially deprive the buyer of what he expects under the contract, the buyer may take the above-mentioned measures: requiring the delivery of substitute goods or declaring the contract avoided.

It is out of the following consideration③ why the buyer may require the seller to deliver substitute goods only when the inconformity amounts to a fundamental breach of contract: if the seller has to deliver the substitute goods and handle the rejected goods,④ the expenses are often higher than the losses that the buyer would have suffered to receive the unsatisfactory goods. Therefore, the Convention provides that if the inconformity is not serious enough as to constitute a fundamental breach, the buyer cannot apply the remedy of requiring delivery of substitute goods, he can just resort to other remedies such as claiming damages or requiring the seller to repair the goods, which will be explained later.

---

① 依…而定 ②不符 ③出于以下考虑 ④退货

To declare the contract avoided can be applied only when fundamental breach of contract occurs. If the inconformity is not serious enough to constitute such breach, the buyer may allow an additional period of time for the seller to repair the goods so that they can conform with the contract. If the seller cannot repair the goods within the period fixed by the buyer, or he simply declares that he will not take any remedial measures within the period, the buyer may declare the contract avoided.

2) In case of non-fundamental breach the buyer may require the seller to repair the goods or reduce the price of the goods.

The Convention provides that the buyer may require the seller to remedy the lack of conformity by repair, unless this is unreasonable having regard to all circumstances. The provision is often applied when the buyer thinks that the repair work will not lead to unreasonable expenses or inconvenience and that the goods, after repair, will be suitable for its original purpose.

Sometimes, the buyer does not require the seller to repair the goods, when they do not conform with the contract. Instead,[①] he requires the seller to reduce the price of the unsatisfactory goods. The Convention provides that the application of the measure may be adopted whether or not the buyer has paid the price. The price is reduced in the proportion[②] as the value

---

① 而是 ②以…为比例

that the goods actually delivered had at the time of the delivery bears to the value that the contracted goods would have had at that time. However, if the seller remedies the inconformity, or if the buyer refuses the seller's offer for such remedy, the buyer may not reduce the price.

It must be emphasised[1] that whether the inconformity amounts to fundamental breach of contract or not, the buyer must notify the seller such inconformity within a reasonable period of time, or he will be deprived of the right to claim that the goods do not conform with the contract. If the buyer does not notify the seller of the inconformity of the goods delivered within two years starting from the date he has received the goods, he may in no way claim that the seller has delivered the defective goods unless the validity time of the contract is more than two years.

Remedies for Breach of Conrtact by the Buyer

The buyer has two major obligations: one is to pay the price and the other is to take delivery of the goods. If the buyer fails to perform these obligations, the seller may take the following remedial measures:

1. To require the buyer to perform his obligations

The Convention provides that the seller may require the

① 强调

buyer to pay the price, take delivery or perform his other obligations, unless the seller has resorted to a remedy which is inconsistent with this requirement (Art. 62). This is the measure of specific performance, which is restricted by Article 28 of the Convention. As the provisions on specific performance based on[①] different legal systems are varied and even contradictory, sellers in general[②] avoid the application of the remedy.

2. To Claim damages

When the seller resorts to such remedy, the damages he claims is equal to the loss (including interests) caused by the breach of the buyer, and the damages may not exceed the loss which the buyer foresaw or ought to have foreseen at the time of the conclusion of the contract. To be exact,[③] if the seller has resold the goods in a reasonable manner, he may get the sum of money equal to the difference between the contract price and what he can obtain from the reselling transaction minus[④] the compensation[⑤] for other losses as the consequences of the buyer's breach. If the seller does not resell the goods after he declares the contract avoided, he may get the sum equal to the difference between the contract price and the current[⑥] price at the delivery place minus other damages caused by the breach. If the buyer delays the payment of the price, the seller may require the buyer to pay the loss of interest.[⑦]

① 基于 ②通常 ③确切地说 ④减去 ⑤ 补偿 ⑥现在的 ⑦利息

3. To declare the contract avoided

According to the Convention: on the following two occasions the seller may declare the contract avoided:

1) if the failure by the buyer to perform any of his obligations under the contract or the Convention amounts to a fundamental breach of contract:

2) if the breach by the buyer does not amount to a fundamental breach, and the buyer does not perform his obligation to pay the price or take delivery of the goods within the period of time fixed by the seller, or he declares that he will not do so within an additional period so fixed.

In international trade practice, it is often difficult to judge whether a breach of contract is a fundamental one. It is practical that the seller sets an additional period of time for the buyer to perform his obligations. If the buyer still refuses to perform his obligations within the period, the consequence is inevitable that the seller delares the contract avoided and claims damages at the same time①. However, in setting the time of grace,② the seller must strictly follow the rule, i. e. he may not resort to other remedies during the period, or he will be deprived of the right to declare the contract avoided, though he still retains the right to claim damages.

---

① 与此同时 ②宽限期

CHAPTER SIX

Export And Import Procedures In China

In an international sale, both the exporter and the importer must respectively perform their duties or obligations as seller and buyer, and the party that fails to do so will have to suffer the serious consequences; for the sales contract becomes a legal document① once it is effectively formed. This chapter gives an introduction to the major conventional② procedures adopted by the Chinese foreign trade corporations in their export and import practice. As the obligations of the two parties are set forth vis-a-vis the exporter and the importer adopt procedures different from each other in the opposite direction. Thus, the chapter introduces the procedures for export and those for import in a separate section.

Export Procedures

Most of the sales contracts signed between Chinese foreign trade corporations (FTCs) with their foreign counterparts are

---

① 法律文件 ②常规的

CIF (cost, insurance, and freight) and CFR (cost and freight) contracts which are generally paid by means of* sight letters of credit[①]. To perform such contracts generally consists of the following procedures: preparing goods for shipment, asking the buyer (importer) to open a letter of credit (L/C)*, examining and amending the L/C[②], booking space or chartering vessel for carriage of the goods, clearing goods through the customs[③], getting paid after documentation[④].

1. Preparing goods as required under the contract

After the contract is formed, the seller makes arrangement with the factories for production of the goods. He must make sure that the goods conform with the contract in quality, quantity, specification, packing etc. If the goods must fit for some particular purpose, under the contract, the seller should make sure that the goods fit for such purpose[⑤] in China, almost all FTCs have a department in charge of the supply of goods. Preparing the goods is the starting point[⑥] for export. If the exporter receives the L/C, or shipping arrangement[⑦] is set, but the goods are not available, the exporter may face a very troublesome[⑧] situation.

2. Examining and amending the L/C

This procedure is preceded[⑨] by asking the importer to

---

① 即期信用证 ②审证和改证 ③出口通关 ④制单 ⑤部门 ⑥起点 ⑦装运安排 ⑧麻烦的 ⑨位于…之前

open a letter of credit. Opening an L/C is an important obligation for the buyer, but in practice it often occurs that the buyer does not open the L/C by the time provided in the contract. Therefore, the seller should, at a suitable time, remind or urge the buyer to open an L/C so that the contract can be performed smoothly. The seller may do so by means of sending a letter or telegram or he may seek① help from the bank or some institutions of the Chinese government in foreign countries.

After the L/C has reached the exporter, he must examine it very carefully. Four essential points must be taken into consideration② in the examination of an L/C coming from a foreign country. We must see a. whether it is in compliance with our foreign trade policies③; b. whether the exporter has the assurance of getting paid by this L/C; c. if it comes from a state which has signed a trade agreement④ with the Chinese government, whether it is in compliance with such agreement; d. whether the credit terms⑤ in the L/C conform with those in the sales contract. Generally speaking, the examination of an L/C embraces the following points:

1) Making clear⑥ the credit-worthinese⑦ of the opening bank. This may be an important safeguard⑧ for the exporter against non-payment, or late payment.

---

① 寻求 ②考虑在内 ③外贸政策 ④贸易协定 ⑤信用证条款 ⑥弄清 ⑦信用状况 ⑧确保

2)Examining the nature of the L/C and the liability of the opening bank. Generally, we require that an L/C from a foreign country be irrevocable[①]. If it does not expressly set out "irrevocable", the L/C may be regarded as a revocable one[②]. In order to get payment safely, when there are provisions in an L/C like "this bank may exercise the right to get recourse", or other provisions that limit the liabilities of the opening bank, we generally do not accept such an L/C.

3)Cheking the sum of money. The amount of money in the L/C must be identical with that in the contract. If there is a "more-or-less" clause[③] in the contract, the amount of money for the excess[④] or deficiency[⑤] must be provided in the L/C.

4)Making sure that there must be an interval[⑥], say 15 days, between the time of shipment and the validity time of the L/C . This is done because the exporter should have enough time for documentation and getting paid. This place for negotiation must be specified to be in China. If the L/C arrives so late that the exporter cannot ship the goods by the time required under the contract, the exporter must telegraph the importer to extend[⑦] the shipping and validity time as soon as possible.

5)Examining other credit terms such as quality, quantity, specificatons, packing etc. If these terms do not conform with

---

① 不可撤消 ②如信用证上没有确标明是不可撤销的,即可视为是可撤消的 ③溢短装条款 ④超出部分 ⑤不足部分 ⑥一段间隔 ⑦延长(期限)

those in the contract, we should not accept the L/C unless the importer amends the L/C according to our request.

6) Examining the documents that the exporter should supply as per the stipulations of the L/C, including the specific ways to fill out[1] the documents.

The exporter should also compare other credit terms with the contractual ones, if he finds any inconformity which he cannot accept, the exporter must ask the importer to amend the L/C. If the amended L/C turns out[2] to be still unsatisfactory, the exporter may ask the importer to amend the L/C again, until the credit terms conform with the contractual provisions.

3. Chartering proper means of transportation

The choice of means of transportation may be determined by a number of factors: characteristics[3] of the goods, amount of cargo[4], freight, destination, etc. In international trade, most of the goods are carried by sea going[5] vessels, for ships take a lot more cargo at a time[6], and the freight charge[7] is lower than that of other modes of transportation. But there is an obvious disadvantage: it takes much longer time for ships to get to the given[8] destination. Therefore, when we need faster dispatch, we may ship the goods by rail[9] or by air. If the exporter decides to dispatch the goods by ship, he may have two options: a. to book space on a liner[10] if the goods are of small quantity or

---

① 填写 ②结果是 ③特点 ④货物 ⑤海上航行的 ⑥一次 ⑦费用 ⑧所指定 ⑨火车 ⑩班轮

sundry goods[①], b. to charter a whole ship if the quantity of goods is too big for a liner or need to be carried by a special sea vessel, like a tanker[②] or a bulk carrier[③].

Before the goods are loaded on board a carrying vessel, the exporter has to apply to the Customs and the Commodity Inspection Bureau for inspection and customs declaration[④]. If it is a CIF contract, the exporter must* take out insurance[⑤] from an insurance company so that he may get an* insurance policy or a certificate[⑥]. After the exporter has gone through[⑦] these procedures, he may start loading the goods, and upon completion[⑧] of the loading work, he should send the importer a shipping advice[⑨] at once.

4. Documentation and getting paid

After the shipment of the goods, the exporter must prepare the relevant documents as required under the contract and the L/C, and submit the documents to the bank for financial settlement. The procedure of documentation is key to international sales, sometimes more important than the goods proper*. If all documents prepared by the exporter are consisent with the provisions in the L/C, the exporter may get paid from the bank even if the goods are lost in transit[⑩]. Besides payment, export documents are evidences for delivery and claim.

---

① 杂货 ②油轮 ③散装货轮 ④报关 ⑤投保 ⑥保险单或保险凭证 ⑦通过(手续) ⑧完成 ⑨装船通知 ⑩如出口方准备的各种单据都与信用证条款相符,则即使货物在运输途中丢失,他也照样能从银行得到货款

When preparing the documents, the exporter should do his best to make sure that "documents are in concord with① one another". The exporter must submit the following documents when applying to a bank for financial settlement.

1) Commercial Invoice. This document states, among other things, the name, the description, and the total value② of the commodity. Its main purpose is for the buyer to take delivery, keep account③ and make payment, and is also the basis on which import or export duty④ will be assessed⑤.

2) Bill of lading (B/L). This is the most important document provided by the exporter. It is issued⑥ by the shipping company⑦ acknowledging receipt of the goods of the exporter, and it is a document of title to the goods. When the importer receives the B/L, he may be regarded as the owner of the goods. Generally, in China bills of lading will be issued by China Ocean Shipping Company (COSCO)⑧ or China Foreign Trade Transportation Company (Sinotrans)⑨, for in most cases Chinese FTCs apply to the two shipping companies for carriage of their goods. Most letters of credit require that a B/L be a "clean, on board" B/L⑩, and the exporter must make sure to comply with the requirements under the L/C.

---

① 与……一致 ②总价格 ③入帐 ④进出口关税 ⑤评估 ⑥制做，发给 ⑦船运公司 ⑧中国远洋运输总公司 ⑨对外贸易运输总公司 ⑩清洁的，已装船提单

3) Insurance policy. The document is needed when the contract provides that the exporter effect insurance①. The goods stated② in the insurance policy must conform with those in the B/L, and the exporter must effect insurance according to provisions under the contract of L/C with respect to③ the kinds of coverage④, and amount of insured value. In practice, insured value⑤ is* 110% of the invoice value⑥.

4) Commodity Inspection Certificate. This is a certificate that certifies the quality and quantity of the goods being in conformity with provisions under the contract. The requirement of inspection varies with the nature and peculiarities⑦ of the goods in international trade. For example, the exporter may just provide a certificate of quality and quantity, or a weight memo if the exported goods are ordinary textile goods⑧ or other light industrial goods⑨. However, when the inspection involves such goods as animal products, herbs⑩ or other plants, a certificate of health⑪ or a sanitary certificate⑫ will be required in addition to the common certificate of quality, quantity or weight.

5) Other documents. Sometimes the contract or L/C requires the exporter to provide some special documents besides the above-mentioned ones, e. g. customs invoice⑬, consular invoice, certificate of origin, etc.

---

① 投保 ②所报的 ③涉及 ④险种 ⑤投保金额 ⑥投保金额通常按发票金额的110%来算 ⑦特性 ⑧纺织品 ⑨轻工产品 ⑩中草药 ⑪健康证明书 ⑫卫生证明书 ⑬海关发票

Import Procedures

When we import merchandise[1] from foreign countries on an FOB basis, we must effect insurance and charter vessel for carriage by ourselves. More importantly, the buyer must perform the two basic obligations: to pay the price and take delivery of the goods.

The import procedures are listed as follows:

1. To establish an L/C with a bank

The buyer must apply to a bank to open an L/C within the period of time as prescribed[2] in the contract. If the contract provides that the buyer should open the L/C after export licence and/or performance bond is available, the buyer should wait for the seller's performance of such duties before he establishes an L/C with a bank. If, for some practical reason, the buyer has to open an L/C before such performance by the seller, the buyer may add such terms as "this credit is effective after the beneficiary[3] presents the export licence and deposits[4] the performance bond"[5]. If the seller proposes[6] to amend the L/C in regard to some terms in the credit, the buyer may negotiate with the seller, and make the amendment on the basis of their agreement reached in the negotiation.

---

① 商品 ②载明 ③出口许可证 ④受益人 ⑤存入(钱) ⑥提议

2. To make shipping arrangement

When the contract is on an FOB basis, the buyer in China is responsible for making shipment arrangement, After the buyer charters the carrying vessel, he must give the seller notice of the date of the ship's arrival at the loading port, so that the foreign seller will have enough time for preparation of shipment. If the buyer anticipates that the shipp he chartered may meet with ① some difficulties in entering the designated port, he may entrust② the seller as his agent to attend to③ the formalities for port entry④.

3. To effect insurance

When we import goods from a foreign country, the goods will go a long way from the place of loading to the destination and may encounter some kinds of hazards⑤ en route⑥. Therefore, if the contract provides that the buyer should effect insurance in the case of FOB or CFR terms, he should take out insurance immediately after receipt of the seller's shipping advice. The People's lnsurance Company of China⑦ is likely to provide the necessary insurance cover.

4. To pay the price and get the title to the goods

For the payment settlement in international trade, the most common method is payment by documentary credit.

---

① 碰到 ②委托 ③处理 ④港务手续 ⑤灾难 ⑥路途中 ⑦中国人民保险公司

There are others the buyer may use, such as documentary collection, deferred payment, advance payment; etc. When the buyer makes payment to the bank, he gets the title document in exchange ①. However, if the documents provided by the seller do not conform with the credit terms, both the buyer and the opening bank have the right to refuse to pay the price. Therefore, it is crucial for the buyer to examine the documents carefully when paying the price.

5. To take delivery of the goods and clear the goods from the Customs

When the goods arrive at the destination port, the buyer or his agent must make timely arrangements of clearance of the goods from the Customs where the goods and the related documents are checked. Upon payment of the duty and/or tax, the buyer can take delivery of the goods. It is absolutely necessary that the buyer should take up the responsibility to inspect the goods. The inspection may take place at the destination port or some inland city, as the case may be, and then the buyer can get an official② certificate of inspection③ as soon as possible. In case any irregularities④ should occur to the goods, the buyer may claim damages on strength of the inspection certificate. Here, the "offical certificate of inspection" refers to one issued by a special institution for commodity inspection which is men-

---

① 作为交换 ②官方的 ③检验证书 ④非常事件

tioned in the contract and recognized in intermational business world. In China that institution is China lmport and Export Commodity Inspection Bureau① which has enjoyed② high commercial reputation③for its service in the field of commodity inspection since the founding of the People′s Republic of China.

A few supplimentary remarks④ are necessary here. The above—listed import and export procedures are typical ⑤of those which have been in practice⑥ for a long time in the national FTCs. Since the implementation⑦ of economic reform, various types of enterprises collectively owned or privately owned, productive firms and technology development institutions⑧ now join in the import and export trade side by side with the state—owned FTCs. In addition to the somewhat standardized business procedures, many enterprises which engage in border trade⑨, baster trade of other flexible forms of countertrade may adopt import and export procedures which differ slightly from what were mentioned above. Their procedures may deviate⑪in varying degrees from these discussed in this chapter. It is probably out of place to elaborate on⑫ these deviations or modifications now. Nevertheless the major steps in these procedures should not be overlooked⑬ and regarded as optional⑭.

---

① 中国进出口商品检验局 ②享有 ③商业信誉 ④补充说明 ⑤典型的 ⑥使用中 ⑦实施 ⑧科技开发单位 ⑨边境贸易 ⑩对销贸易 ⑪偏离 ⑫详尽的阐述 ⑬忽视 ⑭任凭选择(意为可做,可不做)

Before the re-entry of China into the GATT [1], some formalities such as application for quota-allocation, [2]import or export liences or some sort of foreign exchange permit must be performed with care, but most of them would be eventually[3] modified in the foreseeable future. Therefore, they are not specially mentioned or illustrated in this chapter.

① 中国恢复关贸总协定的缔约国地位 ②配额制 ③最后

International Sales Contract

PART TWO

Contents of International Sales Contract

To familiarize ourselves with the contents of an international sales contract may well be the first step towards the grasp of the technique [1] of how to draft[2] such a sales contract. A business executives in foreign trade must acquire such knowledge and skill in order to be well qualified to negotiate vis-a-vis with foreign counterparts, conclude transactions[3] and sign contracts[4] with them. A contract invariably contains a list of respective rights and obligations of buyer and seller[5], so it is imperative for us to be very prudent[6] and thoughtful to make out the contract stipulations[7] as clear and complete as possible, because disputes may arise from ambiguity and incompleteness[8] of the contract stipulations. Arguments and litigation[9] never benefit anyone. Legal expenses incurred during a court case[10] are exorbitant[11]. In the long run[12], not even the party in whose favour a court rules can benefit.

---

① 技巧 ②起草 ③达成交易 ④签订合同 ⑤买方卖方各自的权力与义务 ⑥慎重的 ⑦条款 ⑧不全面 ⑨争议与诉讼 ⑩法庭诉讼 ⑪昂贵的 ⑫从长远的观点来看

A sales contract consists of three parts: preamble, body of contract and closure or witness clause, of which the second part is the most important and constitutes ① the bulk of a contract②. The body of a contract comprises (1) basic terms and conditions③ such as the object of contract, quality, quantity, packing, price, delivery and payment and (2) general conditions such as inspection, erection④, testrun⑤ and operation, force majeure⑥, warranty and remedy⑦, arbitration⑧, and taxes, These clauses will be dealt with in separate chapters hereafter.

---

① 构成 ②主要部分 ③条款 ④安装 ⑤调试 ⑥不可抗力(指人力所不能预防或难以避免的天灾人祸或意外事件) ⑦担保与赔偿 ⑧仲裁

CHAPTER SEVEN

Preamble

Opening paragraph

Simple as it is, the preamble is quite important because it signifies who is buyer and who is seller, and what they decide to do. Preamble is also called the opening paragraph of a contract, which states the nature of and the parties to the contract, coupled ① with the important reference materials, if any like business communications. Somctimes it mentions a certain bilateral trade and/or finance agreement to make clear how to conduct business and settle payments. In this sense, it governs all other stipulations.

The following are usually included in a preamble:

1. "Name of contract" indicates the nature and form of a contract, e. g. purchase contract②, sales contract ③, processing contract④, leasing contract⑤ etc.

---

① 连接 ②购买合同 ③销售合同 ④加工合同 ⑤租赁合同

2. "Time and place of signing a contract" has a close bearing [①] on the jurisdiction[②] of law and the place of enforcing the contract. In a number of countries, settlement of disputes is governed by the law and regulations of the country where a contract is signed. It is, therefore, necessary to have the time and place of signing a contract written at the top on the right hand side of an ordinary contract, though it may be written in the last part (closure) of a big business contract

3. "Names and addresses of the two parties" and their relationship clearly show their identity[③] and formal business addresses both in English and Chinese. When the foreign counterpart has no Chinese name, the foreign name and address are used, of course, whereby[④] all correspondence and documents on business transaction are dispatched[⑥] accordingly by mail or otherwise. It is clear and definite: who is buyer and who is seller; they are, as a rule, called Party A and Party B. If it is a consignment sale[⑦] or exclusive distribution[⑧] sales business, it must be written into the preamble.

4. "Basis of signing a contract" refers to a part of import and export business being concluded in accordance with bilateral trade agreements or letters of intent[⑨]. Moreover, conclusion of import and export business is mostly based on correspon-

---

① 关系 ②管辖范围 ③身分 ④依此 ⑤信函文件 ⑥发送 ⑦寄售 ⑧包销 ⑨意向书

dence, e.g. telegrams, fax[1], messages, business letters, etc., of which specific reference number[2] and date should be indicated. They provide the legal foundation for business contracts.

Diversity of wording[3].

The phraseology[4] of the preamble varies on different occasions and with different lines of trade. Some examples of preamble commonly used in China's foreign trade are given below;

(1)

Purchase Contract

NO. CAC2173/A1/008

Date: Nov. 15, 1989f

Signed at Guangzhou

The contract is made by and between the China National Native Produce & Animal By-product lmport and Export Corporation[5](hereinafter called the Buyers) and the Carolina Leaf Tobacco Company lnc. (hereinafter called the Sellers) whereby the Buyers agree to buy and the Sellers agree to sell the commodity on the terms and conditions stipulated below:

(2)

Sales Contract

---

① 传真 ②编号 ③措辞的差异 ④措辞 ⑤中国土畜产进出口总公司

No.

Date

Signed at Bejjing

The Sellers: China National Metals & Minerals lmport and Export Corporation [1], Er Li Gou, Beijing, cable address: MINMETALS, BEIJING.

The Buyers…

cable address…

The Sellers agree to sell and the Buyers agree to buy the undermentioned[2] goods on the terms and conditions stated below:

(3)

Contract for Ammonia[3] Plant

Contract No. CUA 73733

Date: 8th November, 1989

Beijing

China National Technical lmport Corporation, Beijing, China[4] (hereinafter referred to as "the Buyer") on the one hand and M. W. Kellogg Company, Houston, Texas, U. S. A. (hereinafter referred to as "the Seller") on the other authorize[5] their representatives[6] from both parties to sign the present Contract (hereinafter referred to as "The Contract") under the following terms and conditions:

---

① 中国五金矿产进出口总公司 ②下述的 ③氨 ④中国技术进口总公司 ⑤授权 ⑥代表

(4)

Contract for Gas Turbine Generating Set①

Contract No 71MHP-081

Date of Signature

December 21, 1989

Beijing, China

China National Machinery lmport and Export Corporation② (hereinafter referred to as the Buyer) on the one side, and John Brown Engineering Ltd. Scotland (hereinafter referred to as the Seller) on the other side, through friendly negotiatons, have come to an agreement on the following content, and are signatories③ to the present Contract.

(5)

Rice Contract No. CSR -74-01

In pursuance④ of the Trade and Payments Agreement between the Government of the Republic of Sri Lanka ⑤and the Government of the People's Republic of China signed on 18th December 1972 the Protocal⑥ relating to the Exchange of Commodities between Sri Lanka (hereinafter referred to as the Buyers) and the China National Cereals , Oils and Foodstuffs lmport and Export Corporation⑦(hereinafter referred to as the

① 汽轮发电设备 ②中国机械进出口总公司 ③签约双方 ④执行(意旨履行), ⑤斯里兰卡 ⑥草案 ⑦中国粮油进出口总公司

Sellers), Buyers and Sellers have mutually agreed to sign this contract whereby the Sellers agree to sell and the Buyers agree to buy one hundred and sixty thousand metric tons ① of Chinese Rice subject to② the following terms and conditions:

① 公吨 ②以…为条件

CHAPTER EIGHT

The Object of Contract

Commodity description ①

The object of contract refers to the commodity description, specifications, model (or type), number and quality. Commodity description (or name of commodity) should be spelt out in full and in conformity with international usage. If it is in Chinese, the name should be translated into English or other foreign languages, as the case may be. Sometimes, a commodity like medicine has its technical name and trade name, in such a case it is preferable to use both , because only a trade name might cause confusion. In the case of animals and plants, names based on scientific classification in Latin language can better serve the purpose in addition to their trade names.

Quality

Quality of a commodity can be expressed in specifications,

---

① 商品名称

grade [1], standard, or by sample, sales literature[2], trade mark, brand[3], etc, by which machines, instruments, chemicals, pharmaceuticals[4], metals, minerals, industrial and agricultural products are traded. As to pharmaceuticals, like Tetracycline HCI tables[5] (sugar coated), reference can be made to British (or U. S.) Pharmacopoeia[6] 1973, which provides detailed specifications of the medicine. In some developed countries, the government sets a standard quality for wheat. Trade association of many countries, and international industrial and commercial organizations have set standards of certain commodities such as tin, zinc[7], wolfram[8] and other metals. Standard-tin is traditionally quoted[9] and traded at London Metal Exchange[10]. It is up to the parties concerned to adopt the LME standard as pricing basis[11]. In commercial circles, a large quantity of catalogues[12] and leaflets of industrial products are distributed to the buyers, in which trade marks, brands, model number, specifications, etc. are provided. They can be used in offers and acceptances[13], and written into contracts.

Samples[14]

When description of commodity proves to be inadequate[15]

---

① 等级 ②销售说明 ③牌子 ④药品 ⑤四环素 ⑥药典 ⑦锌 ⑧钨 ⑨报价 ⑩伦敦五金交易所 ⑪报价基础 ⑫商品目录 ⑬成交 ⑭样品 ⑮不足以…

to clearly and fully describe the characteristics of a certain commodity, e.g. its structure and texture [①], and the material of which a commodity is made and so on, we have to use samples especially for art and craft goods, garments[②], light industrial products and native produce. Under such circumstances, it is by seller's samples that the exporters may negotiate and transact business with overseas buyers. However there are times that the buyers send their samples to the sellers for them to make the desired products, that is known as sale by buyer's sample.

The exporter should see to it that the sample he has sent be representative of or identical with[③] the export goods. This is called original[④] or representative sample. In this case, he should not forget to keep some duplicate samples[⑤] on hand to be used for checking when making delivery of the ordered goods or settling disputes over the quality of the goods in question. These duplicate samples must be numbered and kept in good condition to ensure that they will not deteriorate.[⑥]

When we manufacture export goods according to buyer's sample, it must be stipulated in the sales contract that the buyer should be held responsible for infringement, if any, on industrial property right of a third party[⑦]. In big transactions, it is desirable to have the samples sealed by an appointed public

---

① 质地 ②服装 ③与…一致 ④原样 ⑤复样 ⑥变质 ⑦第三方的工业产权

surveyor [1] or jointly by seller and buyer to avoid any dispute over quality in the future.

To safeguard his interest[2] against any possible disputes, the seller may insert[3] the following stipulations in his sales contract: "Quality is considered being about equal to the sample" for commodities like art and craft goods, garments, some of the light industrial products, native produce and minerals.

Specifications

There are times that the seller makes offers[4] by specifications and meanwhile sends samples. Then in the sales contract, only specifications are legally applicable[5] and the sample is given for reference only. For example, soybean[6] of northeast provinces in China is sold by specifications: oil content[7] not less than 17%, moisture[8] not over 14%, admixture[9] 1%, broken bean not over 7%, and samples are given for reference only. It is common practice[10] that in sales contracts of electrical and mechanical goods and precision instruments[11], an appendix[12] is often attached to the sales contract, consisting of blueprints, data sheets and design charts[13] for inspection, testrun and operation, by which the buyer can evaluate[14] and check to see if they conform to performance requirements.

---

① 检验员 ②确保利益 ③插入 ④递盘(报价) ⑤适用的 ⑥黄豆 ⑦含油量 ⑧湿度 ⑨杂质 ⑩惯例 ⑪精密仪器 ⑫附录 ⑬设计图 ⑭估价

Flexibility [1] in quality

Flexibility in quality and specification is often permissible in sales contracts, as a rigid standard for export goods may likely cause trouble owing to its being impracticable, not scientific to put it into practice. For instance, if the exporter sets moisture content of long-shaped white rice at 15% (no more no less), he will find it next to impossible to get a consignment[2] of rice with exactly 15% moisture. It varies slightly with the weather condition prevailing[3]. The moisture content of the rice may be 15% at the time of being packed[4], but when the goods arrive at destination just in monsoon season[5], the moisture content at the time of inspection at destination may be a little bit higher than 15%. Therefore it is usual practice to put moisture content 15% maximum[6], which makes it easier to manage. By the same token, an exporter who deals in cotton or woolen piece goods[7] often offers them with width 47/48″, that means the delivery is acceptable when the width of the piece goods is found between 47and 48 inches. Thus normally the exporter and importer may agree to the max. and min.[8] content measures as the acceptable upper and lower limits[9]. For example, long-shaped white rice is traded by this standard: broken grain 25% max. moisture 15% max. admi-

---

① 灵活性 ②货 ③当时的 ④打包 ⑤雨季 ⑥最大 ⑦羊毛制品 ⑧max=maxinum, min=minimum(最小的) ⑨下限与下限

xture 1% max. In the like manner, sesame is sold by the specifications: oil content 52% min, moisture 5% max. admixture 1% max. This flexible standard works quite well, because it serves the practical purpose of promoting trade.

Major and minor points

A few points are worth mentioning here, when we decide upon quality and specifications. It is preferable for the seller to mention only those relatively important specifications and leave out the minor ones. If the major and minor points are all mentioned in the specifications of a sales contract, it would be too burdensome ① for the exporter to fulfil the task of delivery. After all only the major ones are necessary and decisive to influence the quality or grade of a commodity in question. We must take a realistic attitude towards the specification (or quality) of a commodity in a sales contract. If we make an offer with specifications prescribed② at too high a level and too much in detail, it often causes great difficulty in making the goods for export. Conversely③, if the specifications in our offer are set at too low a level, it tends to depress the price we can obtain, or quite probably tends to turn away the prospective buyers.

Examples

(1)

---

① 负担重的 ②规定,限定 ③相反地

Commodity and Specifications

American Flue-cured Tobacco Leaf ①

in loose leaves CACF 1988 crop

moisture：11-12％

Quality：The goods must be free from plant diseases and insect pests②，especially the Peronospore③ Tabacian Adam

(2)

Name of Commodity：Syrian washed tannery④ sheep wool

Specifications：80％ black，20％ grey，70％yield guaranteed

as per sample delivered to the buyer

(3)

Article：Cocoa Beans⑤ * New Crop

Specifications：First grade with no admixture，not worm eaten⑥(nor wormy)，no mould⑦ and no alien smell⑧

(4)

Name of Commodity：Victorian Wetsalted Meatworks Oxhides⑨

Specifications：Range 30/40 1bs⑩ per piece average 36/38 1bs free of ticks⑪，warble flies⑫，brand marks⑬ or scratches⑭ of any kind，cuts max. 20％，fat and adhering flesh max. 5％，lips，ears，tails，and short shanks⑮ must be cut off.

---

① 烤烟 ②昆虫病害 ③草霜病毒 ④制革厂 ⑤可可豆 ⑥虫蛀的 ⑦霉 ⑧异味 ⑨牛皮 ⑩lb＝pound 磅 ⑪(寄生吸血的)扁虫 ⑫牛绳 ⑬商标名称 ⑭抓伤 ⑮胫骨

(5)

Contents of contract

1.1 The Buyer agrees to buy from the Seller and the Seller agrees to sell to the Buyer 1* (one) set of complete fully mechanized coalface eqiupment① and the related spare parts hereinafter referred to as the "Equipment" and "Spare Parts". Complete details as to delivery, technical specifications, performance and price of the "Equipment" and "Spare Parts" are given in Annex No. 1 to this contract.

1.2 The operation conditions of the coalface of the "Equipment" and "Spare Parts" are set out in Annex No. 2 to this contract.

1.3 The scope for technical documentation, drawings and time of delivery from the Seller to the Buyer are set out in No. 3 Annex to this contract.

1.4 Up to 5 (five) years after the signing of this contract, the Seller is under obligation, at the Buyer's request, to supply the Buyer with the necessary Spare Parts at favorable prices.② (Excerpt from the contract of China National Techincal lmport Corp.)

(6)

Name of Commodity: U.S. No. 2 or better wheat of any class (except white wheat③, durum wheat and mixed wheat) at seller's option④. 1983/84 and/or 1984/1985 crop.

---

① 一整套全部机械化的采煤截面设备 ②优惠价 ③硬质小麦 ④选择

Quality:

1) The wheat supplied by the Sellers should be in conformity with the following specifications:

Moisture: 13.5% maximum

Test Weight[①]: 58 lbs. per Winchester Bushel minimum.

Defects

Heat Damaged kernels[②] 0.2% Max.

Damaged Kernels (total): 4% Max.

Foreign Elements: 1% Max.

Shrunken & Broken Kernels: 5% Max.

Defects (total): 5% Max.

Wheat of other classes:

Contrasting Classes[③]: 2% Max.

Other Classes (total): 5% Max.

2) The wheat supplied by the Sellers must be in good condition, fit for human consumption[④] without unpleasant odour[⑤], free from signs of mould, fermentation[⑥] or deterioration and free from live insect pests such as Rice Weevil[⑦] and Angoumois Grainmoth[⑧].

3) The wheat supplied by the Sellers must be free from the following objects of quarantine[⑨] in accordance with the regulations of the Ministry of Agriculture and Forestry of the Peo-

---

① 容量 ②麦粒 ③对比类别小麦 ④人类消费 ⑤令人恶心的气味 ⑥发酵 ⑦大米象鼻虫 ⑧麦蛾 ⑨检疫

ple's Republic of China [1].

a. Phytophaga Destructor[2] Say.

b. Lolium Temulentum L[3].

c. Sitophilus Granarius[4] (1).

d. Tilletia Contraversa Kuhu[5].

e. Trogoderma Granarium Everts.[6]

f. Necrobia Rufipes[7] (De Gear).

4) In connection with paragraph 3) d Sellers guarantee shipment (s)[8] to be free of Tilletia Contraversa Kuhu ("TCK"). If contaminated[9], the Buyers have the right to reject the shipment[10]. The Sellers have the responsibility to replace at their costs and expenses the rejected cargo(es) with new shipment(s) within 45 days from the date of rejection.

5) The chemical residue[11] of the wheat supplied by the Sellers should not exceed the amount stipulated in the regulations of the Ministry of Public Health of the People's Republic of China:

a. Maximum Arsenic compound[12] content: 1 PPM (1 part per million calculated according to the AS_2O_3 content).

b. No trace of Mercuric Compound[13].

---

① 中华人民共和国农林部规定 ②黑森麦杆蝇 ③毒麦 ④各象 ⑤小麦矮腥穗病 ⑥各斑皮蠹 ⑦椰蝉 ⑧货物装运的 ⑨受污染 ⑩拒收 ⑪残留 ⑫砷化物 ⑬汞化物

c. Max. Phosphides [1]content. (0. 05 part per million calculated according to the PH_3 content).

d. Max. Cyanides[2] content: 5 PPM (5 parts per million calculated according to the HCN content).

e. Max. Malathion[3] content: 8 PPM (8 parts per million). (Excerpts from the contract of China National Cereals, Oils and Foodstuff lmport and Export Corp.)

---

① 磷化物 ②氰化物 ③马拉硫磷

CHAPTER NINE

QUANTITY AND PACKING

Different weight and measure systems

To understand the different weight and measure systems and how to apply them in a sales contract according to the international usage is essential in foreign trade. There are three systems now in use: British, American and Metric systems.① One metric ton equals 2,204 lbs, one British long ton② 2,2401bs and American short ton 2000 lbs. For ramie③, for instance, long ton is often used. For barley,④ the British bushel⑤ is generally used weighing 22.68 kilograms, while the American bushel weighs 21.773 kilograms. Although the difference seems insignificant to some people, yet in foreign trade a transaction may involve a tremendous amount, and if any one makes a mistake in this respect, the loss can be a big sum.

---

① 公制 ②长吨(英国重量单位),等于 2,240 磅,以别于美国的每吨 2,000 磅的短吨 ③苎麻 ④大麦 ⑤蒲式耳

Various kinds of weight

Moreover, we should be aware that there are various kinds of weight. Gross weight [①] means net weight[②] (weight of the goods) plus tare weight,[③] when the goods in a sales contract are of low value, the delivery is likely based on gross weight, i. e, gross for net. [④]But as often as not[⑤], net weight should be used, then tare weight should be deducted from the gross weight. However when a shipment comprises thousands of bags, in order to save labour and time, average tare, or customary tare[⑥] or computed tare, is used instead of actual tare according to different customs in certain trades. In the case of wool and silk, conditioned weight[⑦] is adopted. To ascertain the weight of a shipment of wool, the seller will dry the goods i. e. with practically no moisture content, and add the standard moisture to it, then he can get the conditioned weight.

More or less clause

For goods shipped in bulk[⑧], the more or less clause often appears in a sales contract, e. g. a shipment of 15,000 metric tons of soyabean 5% more or less at seller's option. When the seller is the charterer[⑨] of the carrying vessel, this clause is used

---

① 毛重 ②净重 ③皮重 ④以毛作净 ⑤往往 ⑥习惯皮重 ⑦公量（用科学方法抽去商品中的水分，再另加标准含水量所求得的重量） ⑧散装 ⑨租船人

to make it easier for shipping arrangements. It is applicable to commodities like timber, cereals, oils and the like; the percentage in the more or less clause varies from transaction to transaction. It may be as high as 10% or as low as 2%. Practical experiences tell us that it is advisable for the seller to insert the more or less clause at seller's option in his sales contracts for the above-mentioned commodities, so as to avoid any possible inconvenience in making delivery.

Packing specifications ①

Generally, the way of packing and the material used for packing known as packing specifications are regarded as a basic term of a sales contract. If the sellers fail to comply with the basic term, the buyer is entitled to reject the goods and lodge a claim② against the seller. The outer packing③ is designed to protect the goods, facilitate transportation storage and count reduce freight and storage charges④. Shipping marks⑤ and indicative marks⑥ should be stencilled⑦ legibly on the outer packing. The inner packing⑧ or packaging has additional functions to prettify the commodities and to serve as advertisements. It is especially important when the goods are put on the shelves or on display in show-rooms in the supermarkets. Doubtless, beautiful and attractive package can influence the customers' choice

---

① 装箱明细单 ②索赔 ③外包装 ④减少储运费 ⑤运输标志(唛头)
⑥(包装储运)指示标志(一般用图案或文字表示) ⑦用模板印刷 ⑧内包装

and thus the sales of the said goods.

An important condition

The sellers must attend to the packing specifications in every detail to avoid any possible dispute. Any remissness [1] may constitute breach of contract[2]. A case in point was the decision of British Law Court. An English firm imported a consignment of canned fruits from an Australian exporter. According to the sales contract, canned fruits should be packed 30 tins to a wooden case. When the shipment arrived at the destination, it was found that there were 24 tins to a wooden case, whereupon the buyer rejected the goods, on the ground that the seller made a breach of contract. The buyer won the lawsuit[3], because packing is a basic term of a contract. Preferably, a seller should state in the stipulation of a sales contract that he has the option to decide on packing specifications. However, it is sound practice[4] for a seller to consult with his trade counterpart as to what packing is required, and it should be explicitly written into a sales cotract.

Examples of simple packing specifications

1. For woollen piece goods: in wooden cases containing 30 pcs of 40 yards each.

---

① 疏忽 ②违约 ③诉讼 ④可靠的作法

2. For cotton: in press-packed bales [1] of 400 lbs net each.

3. For vegetable oil: in iron drums[2] of 25 kgs net each.

4. For ground nut[3]: in gunny bags[4] of 60 kgs net each.

5. For Oulong tea: in international standard tea boxes, 24 boxes on pallet, 10 pallets in a FCI container[5]

An example of complex packing specifications. --Excerpt from the Contract between China National Technical Import Corporation (buyer) and M. W. Kellogg Co. U. S. A (seller) is appended hereunder.

Example

Packing and Marking

1) All "equipment and materials" shall be carefully and properly packed in the appropriate conditions so as to withstand[6] long distance ocean and inland transportation and numerous handlings[7], especially due attention shall be paid by the Seller to preventing damage from moisture, rain, rust, corrosion[8] and shock, and taking protective measures according to the different characteristics and requirements of the goods in order to insure their safe arrival at the site of the Contract plant. If any "equipment and materials" be damaged or lost due to improper packing [9], the Seller shall be responsible for repair and or replacement.

---

① 扎捆成包 ②圆桶 ③花生 ④麻袋 ⑤整装集装箱(指所装货物均属于同一托运人或同一收货人的集装箱) ⑥经受住 ⑦多次装卸 ⑧侵蚀 ⑨包装不妥

2) Loose packed accessaries[①] to be packed in cases or in bales shall also be labelled by the Seller indicating the contract number[②], name of main machinery, name of accessaries and its position number of the relative assembly drawing[③]. Spare parts should be marked with the word "spare parts" besides the above particulars.

3) The Seller shall mark the following on each package on the four adjacent sides with indelible[④] paints in conspicuous[⑤] not less than 5 centimeter English printed wordings:

A. Contract No:

B. Shipping mark:

C. Name of equipment and item No:

D. Case No. or bale No:

E. Consignee[⑥] code:

F. Port of destination[⑦]:

G. Gross/net weight: (in Kg.)

H. Measurement: Length, Width, Height (in MM.)

I. Centre of Gravity[⑧]. (in the case of packages weighing more than 2 metric tons each)

Should the package weigh 5 (five) metric tons or more, the case should be marked on the two opposite sides adjacent to the cover of the package to show appropriate international trade practice marks in order to facilitate the loading, discharge and

---

① 散装的附件 ②合同编号 ③有关装配图 ④去不掉的 ⑤明显的 ⑥收货人 ⑦目的港 ⑧重心(包装用语)

handling[①].

In order to prevent losses due to breakage[②] of the package, the machinery and equipment inside the package should be marked by the Seller with contract number and case number.

Each case of the goods supplied by the Seller should be conspicuously marked in English with "Handle with care", "Right side up", etc, and with other appropriate international trade practice marks according to the characteristics and features of the goods as well as requirements different for transportation, loading and unloading the goods. Regarding the unpacked goods, metal label with markings as stipulated above should be put on each of them, or the above said marks with indelible paint should be put on both ends of each package.

4) In each case there shall be enclosed the following documents

A. Unpriced packing list in duplicate;

B. Detailed assembly drawing of machinery and equipment in duplicate;

C. Relevant Certificate(s)[③] of quality in duplicate[④].

5) The design and technical documents delivered by the Seller must be properly packed to withstand numerous handlings, long distance transportation and for protection against moisture and rain. The surface and inside of each packing should be marked with the following in English:

---

① 装卸与搬运 ②破损 ③证书 ④两份

A. Contract No:

B. Shipping mark:

C. Consignee:

D. Destination:

E. Weight (in Kg.):

F. Case/bale No.: Each parcel of the Technical Documents should contain 3 (three) copies of a detailed list of the contents. (Excerpts from the contract of China National Technical Import Corp.)

CHAPTER TEN

Price

Varieties of export price

In foreign trade there are various prices for the same commodity. Granting that the cost of a certain commodity is the same ex-factory ①, the seller will quote you different prices according to the point of delivery. The same price, say ₤5000 per metric ton, would change, if a businessman wants the goods to be delivered at the port of destination instead of at the port of shipment. The seller will pay more for the transportation of goods over a long distance than for a short distance; and there is also a difference as to insurance. Therefore, one can, in no case, get a quotation without delivery terms② or trade terms as they are so called in the Incoterms③ 1990. There must be a definite indication in a quotation sheet④ or a sales contract, defining⑤ what delivery terms the price is based upon. That is why we must make a conscientious study⑥ of the Incoterms 1990.

---

① 卖方工厂交货价 ②交货条款 ③国际贸易条件解释通则 ④报价单 ⑤详细说明 ⑥仔细研究

This pamphlet is to set up international rules with a view to uniform interpretation of the chief terms ① used in a sales contract and do away with the uncertainties of varied interpretations of the same term in different countries. To go into details of the Incoterms here may not be very appropriate; but it is a matter of great importance to get familiar with and to be able to apply them in business discussion. Briefly for ocean and waterway transportation, the three popular trade terms i. e. FOB②, CFR and CIF are used, while FCA③, CPT④ and CIP⑤ are used for multi-modal transport⑥ and other modes of transport. They clarify the division of expenses, risks and responsibilities⑦ between seller and buyer.

A table is appended hereunder:

Mode of Transport and the Appropriate Incoterms 1990

Any Mode of Transport including Multi-modal	1. EXW Ex Works (…named place) 2. FCA Free Carrier (…named place) 3. CPT Carriage paid to (… named place of destination)

① 一些主要条款的统一解释 ②装运港船上交货价(离岸价) ③货交承运人(…指定地点) ④运费付至(…指定目的地) ⑤运费保险付至(指定目的地) ⑥多式联运 ⑦费用,风险,责任

	4. CIP Carriage and Insurance Paid to (…named place of destination) 5. DAF Delivered at Frontier (…named place)[①] 6. DDU Delivered Duty Unpaid (…named place of destination)[②] 7. DDP Delivered Duty Paid (…named place)[③]
Air Transport	8. FCA Free Carrier (…named place)
Rail Transport	9. FCA Free Carrier (…named place)
Sea and Inland Waterway Transport	10. FAS Free alongside Ship (port of shipment)[④] 11. FOB Free on Board (port of shipment) 12. CFR Cost and Freight (destination) 13. CIF Cost Insurance and Freight (destination)

① 边境交货(…指定地点 ②指定目的地未完税交货(…) ③完税交货(指定目的地) ④船边交货

14. DES Delivered Ex-Ship (destination)[1]

15. DEQ Delivered Ex-Quay (destination)[2]

How to choose proper trade terms

In the course of business negotiation, the following points merit our attention:

1) When quoting our delivery terms[3], we should take into consideration[4] the available tonnage[5] of our shipping capability[6], since the China Ocean Shipping Company has possessed a large fleet of merchant vessels and the China National Chartering Corporation[7], more often than not, charters a number of foreign ships. We should try our best to make use of these ships hence for big business transactions, we prefer FOB for our imports and CIF for our exports[8].

2) When the freight market is strong with an upward tendency[9], we would quote FOB for exports rather than CIF. However if the customer insists on CIF terms; to accommodate his request, it is advisable for us to adjust our price to include the compensation for future increase in freight rates[10]. Conversely we should ask for CIF terms for our imports under such circumstances.

---

① 目的港船上交货 ②目的港码头交货 ③交货条件 ④考虑 ⑤吨位 ⑥运输能力 ⑦中国租船公司 ⑧以FOB价进口,CIF价出口 ⑨上升趋势 ⑩运费率

3) The rates of loading and unloading expenses vary from country to country. When the rate of loading expenses is relatively high at a certain foreign port, we should ask for FOB Stowed and Trimmed ① for our imports. When we export, Ex-ship's hold② is more desired than CIF because it explicitly requires the foreign buyer to pay for the unloading expenses. All this refers to shipping full load cargo and does not apply to freight charges of liners.③

4) Under CIF terms, the seller is obligated to arrange insurance and pay insurance premium④. It is provided for in Incoterms 1990 that the goods should be covered on FPA terms⑤ at 110% of the invoice value⑥. However, sometimes the buyers request WPA insurance⑦ instead of FPA and occasionally demand inclusion of War Risks⑧ or other special risks⑨ in insurance coverage⑩. There are times when buyers in some Asian countries intend to better protect his cost and profit and require the insured value to be 150% or anywhere more than 110% of the invoice value. How to cope with such a situation?

In view of the limited protection offered by FPA terms, it is deemed necessary that the CIF buyer, when the contract is made, requires the seller to get more extensive cover, but it must be made clear in the contract that the additional expenses

---

① FOB 理舱与平舱价 ②目的港船舱交货 ③班轮运费 ④保险费 ⑤按平安险条款保险 ⑥发票价 ⑦水渍险 ⑧战争险 ⑨特殊附加险 ⑩险种

thus incurred shall be for the buyer's account [1].

5) Under CIF terms, it is the seller's responsibility to book shipping space[2] in the case of relatively small consignment, i. e. less than a shipload[3], or to charter a tramp vessel[4] in the case of shipload cargo and pay the freight up to destination. If the buyer requires the seller to ship his goods on board of a designated vessel of a certain type, nationality, class, age, etc., how does he cope with this request? From the legal point of view, the seller has the right to decline the buyer's request as such. Notwithstanding[5] that, the seller accommodates[6] the buyer's request provided that this arrangement is entirely feasible[7] from the seller's point of view and does not add anything to his transportation cost.

Variants of CIF terms

Under CIF terms, the seller shall pay the freight, but whose responsibility it is to pay unloading expenses for shipload cargo at the port of destination is to be decided according to the custom of the port. At some ports, it is the responsibility of the shipowner to pay unloading expenses; at some others, the seller has to pay the additional expenses incurred for moving the cargo from ship to wharf godown[8] and from godown to trucks;

---

① 由买方支付 ②订舱 ③船货(整船) ④不定期货船 ⑤尽管 ⑥接纳,通融 ⑦可行的 ⑧码头仓库

but sometimes the situation is quite different, these expenses should be borne by the buyer alone. Therefore, it is equivocal which party shall pay the unloading expense under CIF terms, the seller or the buyer. For this reason, the following CIF variants are introduced to clarify the doubtful points:

a. CIF Liner terms ①

The unloading expenses will be for the account of the party who pays the freight, i. e., the seller under CIF terms.

b. CIF ship's hold

The buyer is to pay all unloading expenses when the goods are discharged from the ship's hold to the wharf.

The risks pass from seller to buyer in the same manner as under CIF terms, i. e., at the time when the goods have effectively passed the ship's rail. ②

Quoting export prices

A price in a sales contract consists of four elements: name of foreign currency ③(rarely in domestic currency), unit price④ (in dollars and cents), trade terms (e. g. FOB, CIF...) and measure unit⑤ (e. g. ton, piece, dozen...). Unit price and total value should be in the same curreny. Oftentimes⑥, the capital letters are used for the total value right behind the Arabic figures.⑦If the price is not firm and fixed⑧, it should be so stated

---

① CIF 班轮条件 ②船舷(指船舶的船内与船外的分界线) ③外币名称 ④单价 ⑤衡量单位 ⑥经常 ⑦阿拉伯数字 ⑧不是实盘

in the contract, and will be adjusted according to certain indexes or criteria[1]. For exports to those countries with which China has signed bilateral trade and payment agreements, we should see to it that trade terms and currency used in the sales contract be in conformity with the agreement. For instance, where the agreement stipulates insurance to be effected by the importer, we must not adopt CIF terms. It should be pointed out that when FOB is adopted in the sales contract for our imports, we must be careful about the division of expenses[2], risks and responsibilities between the two parties. We may choose the appropriate one from the following: "FOB under tackle[3]", "FOB tackle released", "FOB stowed" or "FOB stowed and trimmed".

Escalation clause[4]

The currency problem is a complex one. Sometimes we must comply with the stipulations of the existing bilateral trade agreements, if there is no rigid stipulation concerning the currency in the agreement, the seller has the right to choose. Generally, the hard currency[5] is more desirable than the soft currency[6] If the currency used in a sales contract is a soft one, which is likely to depreciate[7], the seller can make a proposal to

① 指数或标准 ②费用的分摊 ③FOB 吊钩的分摊 ④合同滑动条款
⑤硬通货 ⑥软通货 ⑦贬值

insert an escalation clause. It is designed to safeguard the seller's interest, in case the currency used in the contract like US Dollars actually depreciates as against the strong currency like German Marks [①] at the time of payment. This is quite similar to the payment clause that the money of account[②] is US dollars and the money of payment is German Marks. The ratio between these two currencies at the time of signing a contract is most likely different from the ratio at the time of payment. Payment is made in German Marks or an equivalent amount of US dollars according to the exchange rate[③] at the time of payment, so that the depreciation of US dollars would not affect the seller's interest. In other words, the price is to be adjusted according to the new ratio between the two countries at the time of payment. Or alternatively the currency of a third currency is used in a sales contract through negotiation between buyer and seller.

Commission and discount[④]

Sometimes, the price includes commission for middleman[⑤] or is subject to discount. Generally, commission differs from discount in that commission is paid to middleman after the seller has received the sales income, while discount is deducted from the sales price and usually not paid to any middleman.

---

① 德国马克 ②计帐货币 ③汇率 ④佣金与折扣 ⑤中间商

For example:

Unit price: £500 per dozen CIFC2 [1] London = £500 per dozen CIF London including 2% commission.

Unit price: £500 per dozen minus 2% discount = £490 net per dozen CIF London

In theory the amount of commission is caculated on FOB basis, as it is comparatively reasonable, but in practice, it is often determined through negotiation between buyer and seller. Quite frequently, it is based on CIF invoice value. Same is the case with the calculation of discount.

Open price[2]

Under certain conditions, the buyer and seller are inclined to use open price, in other words, the contractual price is to be determined on a future determinable date according to certain criteria. Sometimes, an adjustment clause is included in a sales contract. It is because delivery of the contracted goods to destination is a bit far away, say[3] in 3 or 6 months after the date of contract or even longer. There is a risk of market fluctuation[4] in such a case, owing to unforeseen changes in market demand and supply of the contractual goods in a relatively long time. In this case both buyer and seller are loath to[5] take a chance[6] and therefore reluctant to put a firm and fixed price in a contract.

---

① CIF 含 2%佣金价 ②开口价，指在将来按某一标准定价 ③例如 ④市场波动 ⑤不愿意干 ⑥冒险

Let us look at the price in a sales cotract of China National Minerals and Metals lmport & Export Corporation, Beijing about export of tin to Europe.

Unit price: CIF Rotterdam per metric ton, the price to be the average of the Seller's quotations of the 3- month forward morning session① of quality 99.95% (for 99.95%), 99.90% and 99.85% and 99.75% (for 99.75%) published by the London Metal Exchange in the contracted month of shipment with premium and discount:

99.95% plus£7.00

99.75% minus£5.00

99.90% plus£4.0

99.85% minus£2.00

The above pricing basis serves to minimize the risk of price fluctuation between the time of signing a contract and the time when the contracted goods may be put on the market. In this way, the buyer can pay a price almost the same as if the goods were sold on spot② at destination. This practice is acceptable in business circles.

In the first place, LME quotation is representative of the world market and obtainable almost on every week day, to which both parties are agreeable. The way of calculation of pr-

① 早盘，早市 ②现货(即期)价

ice based on LME quotations is practicable. Also praticable is the time we take as a basic period for calculation of price, e. g. the average of the contracted month of shipment. Where the adoption of a firm and fixed price is ruled out for a specific sales contract, it is essential for the two parties to specify the particular "time" and the particular "place of business"[①], where world market price can be obtained, otherwise disputes might arise as to how to determine the contractual price. Therefore, one should be careful when an open price is used in a sales contract.

As a rule, a firm and fixed price in a sales contract is preferable, because both buyer and seller can be sure of the cost of goods to be traded. For instance, the manufacturer can get to know how much he pays for the raw material[②] of his product.

In order that the seller can get payment right after shipment, under certain circumstances where open price is adopted, an initial price[③] is provided for in the sales contract, whereby the seller can draw a draft[④] on the buyer at the issuing bank[⑤] of an L/C, and negotiate for payment[⑥] in the exporting country. The final price to settle payment will be negotiated between buyer and seller at a later date as specified in the sales contract.

Price of complete plant[⑦]

It is usually the case when a complete plant is bought, the

---

① 说明具体的交易时间与交易地点 ②原材料 ③初步定价 ④开汇票 ⑤开证银行 ⑥议讨 ⑦成套设备

buyer needs proprietary techniques ① and technical documentation for assembly②, erection③, testrun, and operation. The buyer will have to pay for these softwares, and the total value of the complete plant includes the price for technology imported with the equipment. There is no assurance that the buyer can complete the technical work and put it into successful operation without the help of the technicians employed by the supplier. Thus the price clause, in such a case, is much more complicated than that of ordinary commodity trade and requires much skill and knowledge to understand how the price is calculated and paid in instalments④.

Examples

(1)

Contract Value

1. The total value of the Generating Set⑤ with spare parts and special tools to be supplied under this Contract as detailed in Clause l and technical documentation shall be £3,000,000.000 THREE MILLION POUNDS STERING.

The detailed price list for the Generating Set to be supplied under this Contract is set forth in Appendix 2.

2. The total value of this Contract shall be firm and fixed in price F. O. B. British Port including loading charges, charges for best packing suitable for ocean and inland transportation

---

① 专利技术 ②装配 ③安装 ④分期付款 ⑤成套发电设备

and numerous handlings. The above total contract value includes:

1) The value for one set of Gas Turbine [1] with additional equipment£....

2) Total value for five sets£....

3) The value of one set Spare Parts and Special Tools £....

4) The total value for three sets is£....

(2)

Price

1. The lump sum price of the "equipment"[2] and the "materials"[3], proprietary techniques, reproducibles[4], vendor drawings[5], licence[6], knowhow [7] and technical services[8] required for the "Contract Plant" to be supplied by the Seller as per Section 1 of the Contract is US$... (Say: U. S. Dollars... Million only).

2. The price under Subsection I is a firm price.

3. The said price of the "equipment" and the "materials" is for delivery F. O. B. Baltimore, Houston, Galveston, New York, San Francisco port(s), the United States and/or Kobe port, Japan, including charges for appropriate and strong seaworthy ocean and inland transportation packing[9] for numerous

---

① 汽轮机 ②整套设备价 ③原料 ④复制 ⑤设计图纸 ⑥许可证 ⑦技术诀窍 ⑧技术性服务 ⑨牢固及内陆运输

handlings, loading and unloading as well as charges for the preservation, protection and if necessary painting and all other charges incidental to loading on board the carrying vessel assigned by the Buyer.

4. The price for proprietary techniques, technical documentation and designs is for reproducibles and vendor drawings, to be furnished by the Seller as set forth in Annex No. 5①, also the Buyer's right to reproduce all designs, drawings and documents furnished by the Seller under Contract No. CU-7328 and required for the "Contract Plant".

5. The Price does not include the charges for the Seller's technical personnel② who shall be sent to the "Contract Plant" site for service as per Annex No. 9.

6. Unless otherwise specified, both parties shall according to the Contract send personnel to the country of the other party at their own expense.

(Excerpts from the Contract of China National Technical lmport Corp.)

① 附录5 ②技术人员

CHAPTER ELEVEN

Delivery

Delivery and Shipment ①

The delivery clause is an indispensable component part of a business contract. Where, when and how to deliver the goods must be clarified and settled during business negotiation, failing which, no price can be quoted. In foreign trade, delivery means the actual transfer of the goods, usually to the carrier② which is agreed upon by both parties. In this sense, delivery means shipment of the goods; if however, the Buyers take delivery of the goods at the factory (where the goods are produced), then the Sellers do not concern themselves with the transportation agency and hence no shipment. In most cases of import and export business, "delivery" means the same as "shipment" in meaning.

Time of shipment

After the date of delivery or shipment is fixed, the respon-

① 交货与装运 ②承运人(船)

sibility for effecting shipment must be stipulated in the contract, as that involves making various arrangements. Also, unforeseen events might bring complications. C. I. F. delivery stipulates that the Sellers undertake the complete responsibilty[①] of effecting shipment within the specified period of time. If nothing beyond their control happens, the Buyers can be assured that the goods will duly arrive at the port of destination. Conversely FOB delivery entails[②] the responsibility on the part of the Buyers to book shipping space, or charter a carrying vessel, depending upon the size of the cargo. There must be close coordination[③] between the Buyers and the Sellers in order to ensure smooth handling and effecting shipment. The Buyers have many things to attend to, especially when the cargo requires one or more vessels.

A sales contract sets a period of time or a certain date as deadline[④] to effect shipment of the contracted goods. In case the seller fails to make delivery, it constitutes a breach of contract, for which the seller will be held responsible for the loss that the buyer may incur. So the time of shipment must be clearly defined and we should guard against any ambiguity in the shipment clause. For instance, it is inadvisable to use such terms as immediate shipment[⑤] or prompt shipment[⑥], as there is no unified interpretation[⑦] for the above and disputes may arise.

---

① 承担全部责任 ②使承担 ③密切配合 ④期限 ⑤立即装运 ⑥即期装运 ⑦统一的解释

When payment is made by L/C, the date of negotiation[1] is usually set 15 days after the date of shipment so that the seller will have a period of time to complete documentation[2] and negotiate with the bank for payment of the goods. Nevertheless, if time of shipment and time of negotiation in an L/C fall on the same date, we, as sellers, should think twice before accepting such a condition. This arrangement may cause trouble to the seller, resulting in non-payment[3]. For the seller to advance shipment so as to get payment earlier than as scheduled is inapproriate. Since in such a case the buyer will have to make payment earlier than the designated time, which is unfavourable to the buyer from the perspective of financial management[4]. For this reason, the seller should get prior consent from the buyer if he so desires. Sometimes to insert "partial shipment and transhipment are allowed"[5] into the shipment clause may help facilitate the seller's delivery and receipt of payment.

Time of arrival[6]

For a seller to guarantee the arrival of contracted goods at destination on or before a certain date in export trade is unwise, since there is possibility of encountering some unexpected

---

① 议付期限 ②单据交付 ③无力支付 ④财务管理 ⑤分批装运与转运 ⑥货物到达日期

contingencies[①], while the goods are in transit[②]. In case the goods arrive late at destination, i. e., beyond the contractual date, the buyer can exercise his right to reject the shipment even though the seller has received the payment; under such circumstances, the buyer may demand repayment[③]. An apt example[④] was the export of seasonal[⑤] goods for Christmas gifts. The European importer required the Chinese exporter's guarantee that the goods should arrive at destination on or before December 1st to meet the brisk[⑥] demand of Christmas season. The Chinese seller thought that there was plenty of time for transportation from China to Europe. Being eager to conclude this business[⑦], the Chinese exporter promised the buyer's demand, but unfortunately owing to the breakdown of the engine of the carrying ship[⑧], the ship had to discontinue[⑨] the voyage. The seller did everything possible to hire a boat for transhipping the said goods, but it could only arrive at destination just one day later than the contractual date. At that time the market price[⑩] of the said goods plummeted[⑪] and the buyer took advantage of the late arrival as an excuse to reject the goods. It caused considerable loss[⑫] to the seller. This bitter experience taught us not to take a chance like this example.

---

① 偶然的意外事故 ②在运输途中 ③赔偿 ④合适的事例 ⑤季节性的 ⑥兴旺的(意指大量的) ⑦达成这笔交易 ⑧运载船发动机出毛病 ⑨中断 ⑩行市 ⑪暴跌 ⑫巨大损失

Shipping arrangements

In addition to the FOB and CIF terms as set forth in the Incoterms 1990, we should know something about the contract stipulations concerned with shipping arrangements, when chartering a vessel is necessary to the execution of a purchase contract ①.

Under FOB terms, it is usually the Buyers who undertake to charter the carrying vessel within a stipulated time limit in the case of a shipload cargo. They should advise the Sellers, fifteen days prior to② the arrival of the vessel at the port of shipment, of the contract number, name of vessel, its approximate tonnage③, and estimated time of arrival, to enable the Sellers to make preparations for loading the goods. The shipping company's agent④ at the port of shipment must contact the Sellers directly. If, for some reason, the Buyers want to advance or postpone the date of arrival of the vessel, they shall advise the Sellers without delay.

Should the Buyers agree to have the Sellers charter the carrying vessel, it shall be of a nationality agreeable to the Buyers. It shall arrive at the port of shipment within the stipulated time of shipment, and the Buyers' agreement to the principal terms⑤ of the charter party⑥ must be obtained beforehand. If

---

① 履行购买合同 ②在…之前 ③大约吨位 ④船公司代理 ⑤主要条款 ⑥租船合同

the carrying vessel is delayed for some reason or another, then the goods will be detained [1] at the port of shipment. The Sellers will then be responsible for the goods for so long as they remain there. All this means much extra work and shows the need for correctness in every detail[2] when going over the delivery terms of a contract and the content of the charter party.

Seller's responsibility

In the event of the Sellers' failure to effect shipment upon the arrival of the vessel at the loading port, the dead freight[3] and demurrage charges [4] thus incurred shall be for the Sellers' account[5]. All expenses shall be calculated and settled in accordance with the bills and certificates issued by the shipping company or the relevant department. In case the Buyers' vessel fails to arrive at the port of shipment within 15 or 30 days as the case may be after the confirmed loading date[6], the Sellers shall store the goods in a warehouse[7] and pay storage, commencing the 16th or 31st day from the confirmed loading date. The warehouse receipt[8] shall be negotiable for payment instead of bill of lading[9]. The title to the goods[10] is then transferred to the Buyers after storing them in a warehouse but it does not free the Sellers from their obligations under the contract. The Buyers shall bear[11] charges for warehouse and insurance and the

---

① 停留 ②每一细节上的准确 ③空舱费 ④滞期费(意旨延期停泊费) ⑤由卖方负担 ⑥确定装运日期 ⑦仓库 ⑧栈单 ⑨提单 ⑩货物所有权 ⑪承担

Sellers shall be responsible for taking care of the goods in the warehouse and remain under obligation to deliver the goods on board the vessel at their expense and risk, according to the shipping date given by the Buyers.

We must insert those stipulations, or stipulations to that effect into our contract to avoid unnecessary loss and ensure satisfactory execution of the contract. The contents of those stipulations regarding delivery may vary according to our needs and must be agreed upon by both parties. A few examples given in this chapter will show the points we must pay attention to both before and after the signing of a contract.

Insurance arrangement

The delivery terms also have some bearing upon the insurance of the cargo. Under the FOB terms, if it is shipload cargo, the Sellers shall, immediately after the goods are loaded on board ① the carrying vessel, inform the Buyers by cable②, so that they may arrange with the insurance company to cover the risks③. When break-bulk cargo④ is shipped by a liner, the seller is supposed to send the shipping advice⑤ to the overseas buyer soon after he has got the shipping order⑥ from the shipping line⑦, consequently the buyer can arrange for insurance even before the goods are loaded on board. Under the CIF terms, the

---

① 装上船 ②电传 ③保险 ④普通货物 ⑤装船通知 ⑥装货单 ⑦航运公司

Sellers shall act upon the contract stipulations for the necessary insurance, whereas under the CFR terms, the matter of insurance will be taken care of by the Buyers upon receipt of the shipping advice from the Sellers about the shipment in the same manner as under FOB terms.

Special commodities [1]

Should there be inflammable and explosive[2] material among the goods, the Sellers shall notify[3] the Buyers as to names, characteristics, protective measures and special handling of the said goods, in order to prevent accident. As to goods requiring a certain temperature, the Sellers shall advise the Buyers as to special attention required during transit and storage. In U. S. A. the maximum limit of weight and measurement for a case of goods is 40 tons in weight and, 18 metres in length[4], 3.4 metres in width and 3.1 metres in height. The maximum limit in different countries varies according to conditions. Should a piece of equipment exceed the limit, the steamship company may ship it on deck[5] and the Sellers shall take measures to ensure the protection of the equipment.

Transfer of title[6]

Delivery does not necessarily constitute transfer of the

---

①特殊商品 ②易燃与易爆的 ③通知 ④在甲板上 ⑤在甲板上 ⑥所有权转让

title to the goods. There is a clause in the International Contract for Hides[1] No. 15, namely:

"The hides are at the risk of the Sellers until they are delivered on board a steamer or in the case of container[2] shipment (s), if applicable, are delivered to the place of acceptance[3]. Thereafter the Buyers will take the risk for all loss and damage, provided all other Sellers' obligations under this contract have been fulfilled. The title to the hides will pass to the Buyers only after the Buyers and/or their duly authorized agent[4] have carried out the terms of payment. The hides remain property of, and title is vested in[5], the Sellers until such a time as payment has been carried out, whether or not the hides are under Buyers' control..."

It is very important to make it very clear when, how and where the title to the goods is transferred, so that we can get protection of our interests, and define the responsibility on both sides as to who is to pay the expenses and bear the risks.

Frozen ports[6]

One must be careful about shipment clause if the destination is a frozen port. For instance, seaports in Finland and Sweden[7] are frozen ports from mid-December to early April,

---

① 兽皮 ②集装箱 ③接货地点 ④合法授权的代理 ⑤授权 ⑥冻港
⑦芬兰和瑞典的港口

the time of shipment should not be stipulated to be within this frozen season. It is advisable to insert a stipulation in the contract that in case the shipment of goods cannot be completed before the coming frozen season, the seller is allowed to continue shipment when the frozen season is over with the contract price remaining unchanged.

Destination in a land-locked country ①

If the destination is located in a land-locked country, the seller should think twice before quoting a price CFR or CIF inland city like Kabul, Afghanistan②. If he does make such a quotation, the seller is under obligation to take care of transshipping the goods from the sea port to the inland city③, this adding to the transportation cost. Generally, we should refrain from④ quoting CFR and CIF inland city, unless arrangement can be made, such as multimodal combined transport⑤, by which the seller can hand over the goods to the first casrrier and fulfil his obligation of delivery by quoting CPT or CIP instead of CFR or CIF. Thus the seller may very well accommodate the overseas buyer's demand to despatch the goods⑥ to an inland destination. In the choice of delivery terms, the seller should take into consideration the actual transit route⑦ and

---

① 内陆国家 ②阿富汗的首都喀布尔 ③内陆城市 ④制止(意旨,避免) ⑤多式联运 ⑥发货 ⑦确切的运输路线

decide the use of appropriate delivery terms to suit specific situations.

Optional destinations

When there are two or three optional destination ports in the shipment clause of a sales contract for break bulk cargo, it is necessary to stipulate that the consignee (i. e., the buyer) must declare the destination of the cargo--days before its arrival and the option fee ① is to be paid in excess amount under L/C.

It is unwise for the seller to accept such shipment terms as CIF European main ports② or U. S. East Coast, because how to define the above two destinations is subject to③ different interpretations.

EXAMPLES

(1)

Delivery

(1)In case by sea on the basis of FOB terms:

Booking of shipping space shall be attended to by the Buyers' shipping agents, China National Foreign Trade Transportation Corporation, Beijing. The Sellers shall, 30 days before the date of shipment, advise④ the Buyers by cable/letter of the Contract number, commodity, quantity, value, number of pack-

---

① 选港费 ②主要港口(指班轮在特定航线内经常停告的港口) ③取决于 ④通知

age[1], gross weight and date of readiness[2] at the port of shipment for the Buyers to book the shipping space. The Sellers shall bear all expenses, risks of the commodity before it passes over the vessel's rail and is released from the tackle.[3]

(2) In case by parcel post[4].

To be delivered by the Sellers via Sea-Mail[5] or Air-Mail[6] in one lot[7] to Beijing, consigned[8] to the China National Foreign Trade Transportation Corporation, Beijing.

(3) In case by air freight[9].

To be delivered by the Sellers per PIA[10]/CAAC[11] or per AIR FRANCE/CAAC in one lot to Beijing/Shanghai, consigned to the China National Foreign Trade Transportation at the destination.

(Excerpts from the Purchase Order of China National Light Industrial Products Import & Export Corporation[12])

(2)

Terms of Shipment

(1) Terms of FOB Delivery

A. For the goods ordered in this contract, the carrying vessel is to be arranged by the Buyers or the Buyers' Shipping

---

① 包装号 ②备货 ③吊钩 ④邮包 ⑤海运邮递 ⑥航空邮递 ⑦一批 ⑧寄货 ⑨空中货运 ⑩巴基斯坦国际航空公司(Pakistan International Airlines) ⑪中国民用航空总局(Civil Aviation Administ ration of China) ⑫中国轻工业产品进出口总公司

Agent ①, China National Chartering Corporation. The Sellers shall bear all the charges and expenses until the goods are effectively loaded on board the carrying vessel.

B. The Sellers shall advise the Buyers by cable, 30 days before the contracted time of shipment, of the contract number, name of commodity, quantity, loading port and expected date of arrival of the goods at the loading port, enabling the Buyers to arrange for shipping space. Absence of such advice within the time specified above② shall be considered as Sellers' readiness ③ to deliver the goods during the time of shipment contracted and the Buyers shall arrange for shipping space accordingly④.

C. The Buyers shall advise the Sellers by cable, 12 days before the expected loading date, of the estimated layday⑤, contract number, name of vessel, quantity to be loaded and shipping agent. The Sellers shall then arrange with the shipping agent for loading accordingly. In case of substitution of vessel or alteration⑥ of shipping schedule, the Buyers or the shipping agent shall duly advise the Sellers to the same effect.

D. In the event of the Seller's failure in effecting shipment upon arrival of the vessel at the loading port, all losses including dead freight, demurrage fines etc. thus incurred shall be for the Sellers' account. If the vessel fails to arrive at the loading port within 15 days from expiration⑦ of the laydays previously decl-

---

① 船方代理 ②以上指定的时间 ③愿意 ④相应地 ⑤积载期 ⑥更换 ⑦期满

ared by the shipping agent, the storage charges and insurance premium from the 16th day shall be borne by the Buyers. However, the Sellers shall be still under obligation① to load the goods on board the carrying vessel immediately after her arrival at the loading port at their own expense and risk.② The expenses and losses mentioned above shall be reimbursed③ against original receipts or invoices④.

(2) Terms of CFR Delivery:

The Sellers shall undertake to ship the contracted goods from the port of loading to the port of destination on a direct liner⑤, with no transshipment allowed⑥.

(Excerpts from the Contract of China National Metals & Minerals Import & Export Corp.)

(3)

Delivery

(1) All the goods stipulated in Appendix 2 to this Contract shall be delivered in full⑦ by the Seller in two Lots within 8/9 months after the signature of this Contract. The major equipment of the Generating Set shall be delivered in the first lot and the rest of the equipment shall be delivered in the second lot.

Transfer of ownership⑧ of the goods supplied under this Contract shall take place when the goods are effectively loaded on board the carrying vessel at U.K.⑨ Port.

---

① 有责任 ②自负费用与风险 ③补偿 ④凭原始收据或者原始发票 ⑤直达班轮 ⑥不允许转运 ⑦全部 ⑧转让所有权 ⑨United Kingdom(联合王国,指英国)

(2) Loading Port of the goods shall be the British Port of London, and the destination shall be Port of Xingang, China.

(3) The Seller shall notify the Buyer by cable 40 days prior to the loading of the goods, the date of delivery, total weight, total measurements and at the same time send to the Buyer by airmail a detailed list of goods ①(Including case number②, item numbers③, weight, descriptions④, quantity, unit price and total value, measurements and weight of each package and also any special requirements and attention for the goods during transportation and storage). For large packages⑤ weighing over 20,000 kilos and measuring over 12 metres long, 3 metres wide and 3 metres high, the Seller will provide by airmail a sketch⑥ of the cases of the goods, in 5 copies, to assist the Buyer in arranging suitable transportation. The Buyer, within 2 weeks of receipt of the above lists and shipping notice⑦, shall confirm acceptance to the Seller.

(4) When any package weighs over 30,000 kilos and is more than 18 metres long, 3.1 metres high, and 3.1 metres wide, the Buyer and the Seller shall consult each other⑧ for a decision regarding transportation.

(5) The Buyer shall notify the Seller by cable 14 days before arrival at the port of loading, the name of the carrying vessel, estimated date of arrival⑨ at the port and other matters pe-

---

① 详尽的货单 ②每箱编号 ③每件编号 ④说明书 ⑤大件 ⑥略图 ⑦备装通知 ⑧互相协商 ⑨预计到货时期

rtinent to [1] shipment.

(6) After loading the goods, the Seller shall immediately notify the Buyer by cable.

(7) If the Buyer's vessel calls at[2] the loading port and the Seller is unable to get the goods ready for shipment at the time agreed, the demurrage, dead freight and other such expenses incurred shall be borne by[3] the Seller. Such expenses shall be calculated according to the invoices issued by the shipping company.

(8) If the Seller gets the goods ready for shipment at the agreed time and the Buyer's vessel is unable to call at the loading port within 25 days after the estimated date of arrival, the Buyer shall pay for the storage and insurance costs[4] starting from the 26th day.

(9) After the Seller has despatched the technical documents as set out in Appendix 4 to this contract, he shall immediately notify the Buyer, by cable, the dispatch date[5], airway bill[6], the list of documents and weight.

(10) The date on the Bill of Lading shall be regarded as the date of delivery of the Generating Set and technical documents supplied under this contract.

(Excerpts from the Contract of China National Machinery Import & Export Corporation.)

---

① 与…有关 ②到达 ③由…支付 ④保险费用 ⑤发送(邮寄)日 ⑥空运单(指航空公司收到托运人空运货物的单据)

CHAPTER TWELVE

Payment ①

Banker's credit

In every contract for the export of goods, there are four major points in the clause dealing with the payment of the goods: time, mode②, place and currency of payment. The merchantile custom③ has developed certain payment clauses which facilitate export transactions④. The interest of the exporter is to receive payment as soon as possible, and to keep the documents of title to the goods⑤ until payment has been made, or, at least until such a time as he can be certain that his draft has been accepted⑥, while it is in the buyer's interests to postpone payment until he has an opportunity of reselling the goods. The most important of these payment clauses come under banker's credits⑦.

---

① 支付 ②支付方式 ③商业习惯 ④促进出口贸易 ⑤持有货物所有权单据 ⑥承兑(指付款人对远期汇票表示承担到期付款责任的行为) ⑦银行信用证

The common feature of all banker' credits is the buyer' s arrangement to make payment ① to the exporter on delivery of the shipping documents②. On presentation③ of the shipping documents, the banker pays the purchase price, either by accepting a sight draft④ or time draft⑤ or by paying cash⑥. A banker' s credit is in the form of⑦ a documentary credit⑧. The banker is prepared to make the advance⑨ to the exporter because it holds the shipping documents as security⑩ for the advance and, if necessary, can take recourse⑪ to the exporter, as drawer of the draft⑫, and instruct him to make up the loss⑬. The confirmed irrevocable letter of credit⑭ is the type of commercial credit most favourable to the exporter because the opening (issuing) bank⑮ stipulates as below that it will honour⑯ the exporter' s drafts, provided that they are drawn and presented in conformity with the terms of credit⑰.

" We undertake to honour all drafts drawn within the terms of the above credit…"

Exporter' s draft

When an irrevocable letter of credit is confirmed by anoth-

---

① 付款 ②装运单据 ③提示，指持有人将汇票运输单据提交付款人要求付款） ④即期汇票（指汇票上规定付款人见票后即需付款的为即期汇票） ⑤远期汇票（指汇票上规定于将来一定日期付款的为远期汇票） ⑥现金支付 ⑦以…形式 ⑧ 跟单信用证（指凭汇票和单据付款的信用证） ⑨预付货款⑩保证 ⑪追索 ⑫出票人（即签发汇票的人，通常是出口人或银行） ⑬弥补损失 ⑭保兑的，不可撤销的信用证 ⑮开证银行 ⑯兑付 ⑰与信用证条款一致

er bank in the exporting country or in a third country, the seller can get more assurance for payment, since the confirming bank undertakes [1] to honour the draft if the issuing bank fails to do so. Then, what is a draft? A draft or a bill of exchange[2], as defined by the Uniform Negotiable Instruments Law[3] in the western countries, is an unconditional written order, addressed by one person to another, calling on the person to whom it is addressed, to pay on demand[4] or at a fixed or determinable future time, a sum of money to the order of a specified person or to bearer[5]. Thus a draft is useful to the exporter as a means to collect the money from the importer abroad. Under a documentary credit, the banker advances the money and finances the payment for the goods for the importer. More often than not, the importer who applies for the establishment of the credit pays the interest for the advance.

Kinds of credit

Credits can be classified into various types according to their mode of availability[6].

1. Sight credit[7]

The most commonly used type of credit is the sight credit.

---

① 保兑银行承担…责任 ②汇票 ③《统一流通票据法》 ④立即支付 ⑤在将来固定的时候或可以确定的时间支付一定金额给特定的人或其指定的持票人 ⑥用款方式 ⑦即期信用证

It provides for payment to be made to the beneficiary ① immediately after presentation of the stipulated documents and on condition that② the terms of the credit have been complied with. The value date③ for the crediting of the amount to the exporter's account④ will depend on the currency in which the credit was issued. The proceeds⑤ of a Renminbi credit can normally be paid at once. If the credit is expressed in the currency of the importing country or that of some other country, payment generally takes somewhat longer.

In order that the negotiating bank⑥ can get reimbursement sooner than usual, the payment clause may stipulate L/C with T/T reimbursement⑦. T/T stands for telegraphic transfer while M/T for mail transfer⑧, the former can save one week's time for the negotiating bank to receive reimbursement from the issuing bank. Normally it is only after the issuing bank has received the draft accompanied by shipping documents, and examined them that the issuing bank will reimburse the negotiating bank when everything is in order.

2. Acceptance credit or usance credit⑨

The purpose of an acceptance credit is to give the importer time to make payment. If he can resell the goods before payment falls due, he can use the proceeds to meet the draft. In

---

① 受益人(指信用证上所指定的有权使用该证的人,即出口人) ②在…条件下 ③起息日 ④出口商往来帐户 ⑤收入 ⑥议付行(指愿意买入或贴现受益人交来跟单汇票的银行) ⑦电汇(汇付的一种) ⑧信汇 ⑨远期信用证

this way, he avoids the necessity of borrowing money to finance the transaction ①. Having fulfilled the requirements② of the credit, the beneficiary can demand that the usance draft (term bill of exchange) drawn on the issuing bank, correspondent bank or buyer be accepted and returned to him. He can then hand over the accepted bill to his own bank either for payment at maturity or to be discounted, depending on whether or not he wants the cash immediately. Drafts drawn under an acceptance credit usually have a term of 60 to 180 days. There is a time lag and the exporter will wait for payment.

A special kind of usance L/C has been in use in recent years, by which the exporter does not have to wait and can receive payment as if the usance draft were a sight draft. The following are two examples of pseudo③ usance L/C. Please note the wording of the L/C.

1)"We (opening bank) hereby establish our irrevocable L/C for US $.... available by draft at 90 days sight. Discount charges are for account of the granter. We shall pay the draft at sight providing that same was drawn at 90 days after sight and the presenting bank's instruction includes a request to drawee bank to discount the draft remitting the settlement of draft amount at sight."

2)"We (opening bank) have established our irrevocable

---

① 支付这笔支易 ②满足要求(意旨履行条款) ③假的

L/C No. . . . for US $ . . . in your favour available for acceptance of your draft at 120 days. Drawee [1]bank's discount [2]or interest charges and acceptance commission[3] are for account of the applicant[4] and therefore the beneficiary is to receive value for usance draft as if drawn at sight."

3. Deferred payment credit[5]

Under this credit, the beneficiary does not receive payment when he presents the documents, but at a later date specified in this credit. It is often used in the sales of capital goods[6], especialy in the case of a complete plant like a chemical fertilizer[7] plant, an electrical generating set[8], etc. In this way the importer gains possession[9] of the documents (and thereby of the goods or service) before becoming liable for payment[10].

In economic terms, a deferred payment credit is equivalent[11] to an acceptance credit[12], except that in the absence of a draft,[13] there is no possibility of discounting. However, the undertaking to pay established by a deferred payment credit can on certain conditions be accepted as security for an advance.

4. Red clause credit[14]

Under this credit, the seller can obtain an advance from

---

① 付款人 ②贴现:(指以未到期的票据向银行兑换现款,银行从票据金额中扣除买进日至到期日的利息,并收取若干 手续费,把余额以现金付给持票人,叫贴现) ③承兑手续费 ④由开证申请人支付 ⑤延期支付信用证 ⑥资本货物,指用于生产的经济货物,如厂房、机器等) ⑦化肥 ⑧发电厂 ⑨拥有 ⑩必须付款 ⑪与…相同 ⑫承兑信用证 ⑬没有汇票 ⑭红条款信用证

the correspondent bank [1]. This advance is intended to finance the manufacture or purchase of the goods which is going to be delivered under the documentary credit. On receiving the advance, the beneficiary must give a receipt and an undertaking[2] to present the required documents within the validity of the credit. The advance is paid out by the correspondent bank, but it is the issuing bank that assumes liability. If the seller does not present the required documents in time and fails to refund the advance, the correspondent bank debits[3] the issuing bank with the amount of the advance plus interest. The issuing bank, in turn, has recourse[4] to the applicant, who therefore bears the risk for the advance and the interest accrued.

5. Revolving credit[5]

If a buyer has goods delivered to him in instalments at specific intervals[6], payment can be made under a revolving credit, which covers the value of each instalment as it is delivered. The revolving clause frequently specifies the intervals at which portions may be utilized. A revolving credit may be cumulative[7] or non-cumulative. The former refers to the credit of which amounts from unused or incompletely used portions may be carried forward and utilized in a subsequent period. If a credit is non-cumulative, portions not used in the prescribed period[8] ce-

---

① 往来银行 ②保证 ③借记 ④追索(权) ⑤循环信用证 ⑥间隔规定时间 ⑦累计的 ⑧在规定期限内

ased to be available, as do all subsequent portions.

6. Negotiation credit[①]

It is a commercial letter of credit opened by an issuing bank in the currency of its own country[②] and addressed direct to the beneficiary[③]. The letter of credit is usually delivered to the addressee[④] through the intermediary[⑤] of a correspondent bank. The letter of credit empowers[⑥] the beneficiary to draw a draft on the issuing bank, on any drawee stipulated[⑦] in the credit or on the applicant for the credit. The beneficiary can then present the draft to a bank for negotiation together with the original letter of credit[⑧] and the documents stipulated therein. (Negotiation means the purchase and sale of drafts and other marketable securities.[⑨])

Payment of the draft is guaranteed[⑩] by the issuing bank on condition that the documents presented by the beneficiary are in order. The most common variety of negotiation credit permits negotiation by any bank. Rarely, * the choice is limited to specified banks[⑪]. In the case of a commercial letter of credit issued abroad and payable by the issuing bank in its local currency, the payment commission is charged to the beneficiary if the credit amount[⑫] is paid to him in his own currency. This is in contrast to the usual practice for other types of documentary credits.

---

① 议付信用证 ②以本国货币 ③直接开给受益人 ④抬头人 ⑤中间机构 ⑥准许 ⑦指定的 ⑧信用证正本 ⑨证券 ⑩由…担保 ⑪选择限制在某指定银行 ⑫信用证金额

7. **Standby credits**[①]

They are guarantee-type instruments[②] which because of their documentary character are governed by the Uniform Customs and Practice for Documentary Credits[③]. They can be used, for example, to guarantee the following for payment or performance.

--Payment of bills payable[④] after sight

--Repayment of bank advances

--Payment for goods delivered

--Delivery of goods in accordance with contract 3

--Fulfilment of contracts[⑤] for work and materials

8. **Transferable credit**[⑥]

It is designed to meet the requirement of international trade. It enables a middleman who is receiving payment from a buyer under a documentary credit to transfer his claim[⑦] under that credit to his own supplier. In this way he can carry out transactions with only a limited outlay[⑧] of his own funds. The middleman gets his buyer to apply for an irrevocable credit in the middleman's favour. The issuing bank must expressly designate it as "transferable". As soon as the middleman receives the advice, he can instruct the bank to transfer the credit to the supplier (second beneficiary)[⑨]. The documents are forwarded to the transferring bank, which thereupon debits the middleman.

---

① 备用信用证 ②票据 ③《跟单信用证统一惯例》 ④应付的 ⑤履行合同 ⑥可转让信用证 ⑦货物所有权 ⑧费用 ⑨供货人(第二受益人)

The latter hands over his own invoice (made out to the buyer) to the transferring bank and receives the invoice of his supplier in exchange. The middleman is then credited with the amount of this own invoice. The difference between this and the amount shown on the supplier's invoice represents his profit. Finally, the middleman's invoice, together with the other documents, is forwarded to the issuing bank. The basic rule for transferable credits is that it must be possible to obtain payment of the original credit on the strength of the documents presented under the transferable credit.

Thus, the terms and conditions of the transferred credit must be identical with those of the original credit with the following exceptions:

--The amount of the credit and the unit price may be reduced.

--The expiry date ① may be brought forward.

--The period for shipment may be shortened provided that the original credit does not specify a particular date② for shipment.

--The first beneficiary may reqiure additional documents which remain in his possession. Furthermore, the middleman has the right to substitute③ his own invoice for that of the second beneficiary. The difference between the two representing

---

① 到期日 ②特定日期 ③取代

his profit. A transferable credit may only be transferred once. The second beneficiary may not further transfer it unless there is an express provision① to this effect in this original credit, e. g. "transferable twice". This limit on transferability is intended to prevent abuse②. On the other hand, the first beneficiary can transfer fractions③ of the original credit to several suppliers provided that part shipments are permitted. In this case, the transferable credit is also a divisible credit④. This was frequently used in China in the past three decades⑤, when the head office⑥ of national foreign trading corporations concluded sales contracts with overseas⑦ buyers and assigned⑧ the branch offices at sea ports to make shipment of the contracted goods. * The aggregate of these partial transfers⑨ constitutes one transfer.

9. Back-to-back credit⑩

The middleman's bank, accepting as sole security⑪ the first credit issued in the middleman's favour, opens a second credit in favour of the supplier. It will only be prepared to do this if the resultant additional risks can be covered. Thus it will insist on being designated as paying bank for the second credit. It will also insist that a smooth exchange of invoice⑫ is assured, since the original credit in favour of the middleman cannot be utilized on the strength of⑬ the supplier's invoice from the second credit.

---

① 明文规定 ②滥用 ③部分 ④可分割信用证 ⑤十年 ⑥总公司（总部） ⑦海外的 ⑧指派 ⑨分批转让的总额 ⑩背对背信用证 ⑪唯一担保 ⑫发票顺利替换 ⑬凭借

Payment on collection[1] basis

Sometimes, there is no letter-of-credit arrangement by the importer, but the exporter can also arrange with his bank to collect the money from the importer. In this case we call this "payment on collection basis". Under this arrangement, the exporter surrenders[2] the shipping documents[3] together with the draft to the bank at the port of shipment, who will then send them for collection to its correspondent bank at the port of destination. The instructions[4] which the drawer[5] of the draft (the exporter) gives to his bank, may call for delivery of goods, or to be exact, the transfer of the shipping documents upon acceptance of the draft. In this case, a time or usance draft is used; the length of time granted to the importer may* vary from 30 to 120 days[6] after acceptance, so this mode of payment,[7] called D/A or "Documents against Acceptance"[8] is not so often used in our export trade. The seller's instructions may call for immediate payment upon presentation of shipping documents to the importere. We call this mode of payment D/P or "Documents against payment"[9]. On the whole, payment on collection basis is unfavourable to the exporter. Obviously it is unfavourable to the exporter. Obviously, D/P is far better than

---

① 托收 ②提交 ③装运单据 ④指示 ⑤出票人 ⑥从…到…不等 ⑦支付方式 ⑧承兑交单,(指出口人的交单以进口人的承兑为条件) ⑨付款交单

D/A from the point of view of exporters, because they can* retain the title to the goods① until payment is made to the bank who in turn forwards the money to the exporters, while under D/A collection, the exporter relies entirely upon the commercial integrity② of the importer abroad and runs a greater risk of non-payment at maturity.

How to protect seller's interest

It is worth mentioning that under D/P collection, the importer (drawee of a draft) should in most cases pay at sight,③ and less often he is to pay so many days (say 60 days) after sight. At what time the collecting bank④ should make presentation of shipping documents becomes a problem in Latin American and some European countries. There the collecting banks do not present the draft and shipping documents to the buyers' right⑤ after they receive them and would defer⑥ it until the carrying ship of the goods arrives at the destination. Consequently the exporter will receive payment a few weeks later than they are supposed to receive. The delay affects the cash inflow⑦ of exporters and hence their interest. In order to avoid this kind of possible loss of interest, it is advisable to write the following clause in a sales contract: "The buyers should make payment upon first presentation of shipping documents and the draft."

---

① 保留货物所有权 ②商业信用诚实(可靠) ③即期付款 ④代收行 ⑤以买方权益 ⑥推迟 ⑦现金收入

In a few Latin American countries ①, things can be even worse, as the bankers there make no distinction② between D/P after sight and D/A; in other words③, the collecting bank will give shipping documents to the importers when the drawee accepts the time draft under D/P collection terms. Of course, this inappropriate practice④ would cause trouble to the exporter, as it involves the risk of non-payment at maturity after the shipping documents are released⑤ to the buyer.

In the case of usance draft, say 180 days after sight, the exporter may, through negotiation, insert an interest clause⑥ in a sales contract, which stipulates the buyer's obligation⑦ to pay interest on the invoice value for the duration of the draft at... % rate per annum⑧ to the seller. Apparently, this is the way how the exporter protects his interest in the case of a usance draft being used for collection.

Examples

(1)

Terms of payment: *By Confirmed, lrrevocable, Transferable and Divisible Letter of Credit⑨ to be available by sight draft, to reach the Sellers before... and to remain valid for negotiation in China until the 15th day after the aforesaid⑩ time of shipment.

---

① 拉美国家 ②没有区分 ③换句话说 ④不恰当的做法 ⑤放行 ⑥增加利息条款：指汇票上注明支付或兑付票据时须加付利息的条文 ⑦义务 ⑧每年 ⑨保兑的、不可撤销的、可转让的、可分割的信用证 ⑩上述的

(Excerpt from Sales Confirmation ① of the China National Native Produce & Animal By-Products Import & Export Corporation)

(2)

Payment: The Buyers, upon receipt② from the Sellers of the delivery advice③specified in Article 14 hereof④, shall, in 15-20 days prior to the date of delivery, open an lrrevocable Letter of Credit with the Bank of China, in favour of the Sellers, for an amount equivalent to the total value of the shipment. The credit shall be payable against the presentation of draft drawn on the opening Bank and the shipping documents specified in Article 13 hereof. The Letter of Credit shall be valid until the 15th day after the shipment is effected⑤.

(Excerpt from the Purchase Contract of the China National Light industrial Products Import & Export Corporation.)

(3)

Terms of Payment: Upon receipt from the Sellers of the advice as to the time and quantity expected ready for shipment, the Buyers shall open, 20 days before shipment, with the Bank of China⑥, Beijing, an lrrevocable Letter of Credit in fav-

---

① 销售确认书 ②一收到… ③交货通知 ④本文第十四款 ⑤装运完毕 ⑥中国银行

our of the Sellers payable by the opening bank against sight draft accompanied[1] by the documents as stipulated in Clause (9) of this contract.

(Excerpt from the Purchase Contract of the China National Metals & Minerals Import & Export Corporation.)

(4)

Terms of Payment: the Buyer shall open, with a bank to be accepted by both the Buyer and the Seller, an lrrevocable, Transferable and Divisible Letter of Credit, allowing* partial shipments and transshipment[2], in favour of the seller, payable at sight against first presentation of the shipping documents to the Bank of China in China.

The covering Letter of Credit must be opened to reach the Seller before------and to remain valid[3] in China until the 15th day (inclusive)[4] from the date of shipment.

(Excerpt from the Sales Contract of MINMETALS.)

(5)

Payment: After delivery is made, the sellers shall send the following documents, from the Seller′s bank through the Bank of China, to the Buyers for collection.

(1)a. In case by sea:

---

① 随交 ②分批装运与转运 ③保持有效至… ④包括(第十五日)

One full set clean "On Board" "Freight to Collect"/ "Freight Prepaid" ocean Bills of Lading ①, made out to order, ② blank endorsed③, notifying the China Nationl Foreign Trade Transportation Corporation at the port of destination.

b. In case by post:

One copy of Parcel Post Receipt④.

c. In case by air freight:

One copy of clean "On Board" "Freight Prepaid" Air Waybill addressed to the China National Foreign Trade Transportation Corporation at the port of destination.

(2) Invoice 5 copies

(3) Packing list⑤, 2 copies

(4)* Certificate of Quality and Quantity⑥ issued by the Manufacturers⑦, 2 copies.

(Excerpts from the Purchase Order of the China National Light Industrial Products Import & Export Corporation.)

(6)

Payment

Twenty days before the anticipated⑧ shipment date, the Buyer shall open an irrevocable, without recourse Letter of Cre-

---

① 全套清洁已装船，运费到付或运费已付提单 ②凭指定头人（法定收货人），空白抬头 ③空白背书：指转让票据时（如提单等），背书人只在票据背面签名而不指定受让人的一种背书方式 ④一份邮政包裹收据 副本 ⑤包装单、装箱单 ⑥品质、质量合格证书 ⑦厂商 ⑧预期的

dit by the Bank of China, Beijing, in favour of the Sellers, to be advised through a first-class bank① in New York, available against draft/s drawn, in U. S. Dollar at sight in the opening bank in Beijing for 100% invoice value② of each shipment③. The opening bank shall make reimbursement④ payment by T/T against their receipt of the following shipping documents:

1) Commercial Invoice⑤ in quintuplicate⑥.

2) Official Grading and Weight Certificates⑦ in quintuplicate issued by the U. S. D. A. ⑧ Licensed inspectors and Weighmasters certifying that the actual weight and quality of the cargo shipped are in conformity with the stipulations of the Contract (enumerating⑨ the actual percentage of Moisture, Admixture and Natural Weight, etc.)

3) National Cargo Bureau⑩ or U. S. D. A. Licensed Inspector's Health Certificate of ships' holds in quintuplicate evidencing⑪ that the holds⑫ are suitable to receive and carry the wheat.

4) Full set of Clean on Board Ocean Shipping Bills of Lading made out to order and blank endorsed. Charter Party Bills of Lading⑬ to be acceptable Phytosanitary Certificate⑭ in quintuplicate by official U. S. Bodies⑮ of freedom from the inju-

---

① 一级银行(指信用最好的) ②按100%发票价格 ③每批货 ④偿还 ⑤商业发票 ⑥一式五分 ⑦官方分级与重量检验证书 ⑧具有美国农业部发的执照 ⑨例如 ⑩国家货运管理局 ⑪证明 ⑫船舱 ⑬租船契约提单 ⑭植物卫生检验证书 ⑮美国官方机构

rious [1] diseases and live insect pests[2] as well as from the following and indicating the date and nature of treatment[3] and/or fumigation[4] as well as the chemicals[5] and the quantities thereof applied to the shipment. Any wheat treated with chemical agents shall have no harm for human consumption.

a. Phytophaga Destructor Say.

b. Lolium Temulentum L.

c. Sitophilus Granarius L.

d. Tilletis Contraversa Kuhu.

e. Trogoderma Granarium Everts.

f. Necrobia Rufipes (De Geer).

g. Rice Weevil.

h. Angomoumois Grainmoth.

All banking charges outside Letter of Credit opening place shall be for account of the Sellers.

(Excerpts from the purchase contract of the China National Cereals, Oils and Foodstuffs Import and Export Corporation.)

(7)

Payment

(1) All the expenditure[6] incurred under this contract shall be paid in Pounds Sterling[7].

---

① 有害的 ②活的害虫 ③处理虫害的方式 ④(为消毒)而熏蒸 ⑤化学品 ⑥费用 ⑦以英磅支付

(2) The total value of the Contract as stated in Clause 2 shall be paid to the Seller by the Buyer through the Bank of China, Beijing, in the following way and according to the following percentages:

(3) The advance payment shall be 10% of the total value of the Contract, namely ①...

Such payment being made within 30 days after receipt by the Buyer of the following documents presented by the Seller and found in order after examination:

a. Photostat copy② of the Export Licence③ issued by the relevant authorties④.

b. An irrevocable Letter of Guarantee⑤ issued by a British Bank (The Westminster Bank, London) with the buyer as beneficiary for an amount equal to the advance payment of 10% of the total Contract Value (The form of this Guarantee is exhibited in Appendix 6 to this Contract).

c. Pro Forma invoice⑥ in triplicate⑦ equivalent to the total value of the Contract.

(4) Within 30 days after receipt of the shipping advice, as stipulated in* item 3 of Clause 4 of this Contract⑧, the Buyer shall open with the Bank of China, Beijing, an lrrevocable Letter of Credit, payable at sight in favour of the Seller, the equivalent of 80% of the Total Value of this Contract. The Bank of

---

① 也就是 ②直接影印本 ③出口许可证 ④有关当局 ⑤不可撤销的保函 ⑥形式发票 ⑦一式三份 ⑧本合同第四款第三条

China, Beijing, shall pay to the Seller 80% of the Total Value of each shipment within 30 days after presentation by the Seller of the following documents, which, after examination, have been found to conform to this Contract:

a. Original Bill of Lading in triplicate

b. Commercial Invoice, 5 copies

c. Packing List, 5 copies

d. * Quality Control Inspection Clearance Certificate ①, 5 copies (See Appendix 7 for typical certificate).

(5) Within 8 months after delivery of the last shipment of the Generating Sets supplied under this Contract by the Seller, and which has been found up to contract specifications upon inspection by the Buyer and the Seller's representative, the Bank of China, Beijing, shall pay to the Seller 10% of the total Contract value within 30 days against the following documents presented by the Seller which have been found in order after examination:

a. Commercial Invoices, 5 copies

b. Buyer's inspection certificate defined in clause 8.7.

c. An irrevocable Letter of Guarantee for the guarantee period covering 10% of the total Contract value (pounds Sterling...) issued by the National Westminster Bank, London, in favour of the Buyer (Specimen② of the Letter of Guarantee is

---

① 通过品质检验证书 ②样本

exhibited in Appendix 8 of this Contract). The Letter of Guarantee shall be returned to the Seller at the end of the guarantee period. If the guarantee period is extended for reasons on the Seller's side, the validity time of the Letter of Guarantee shall be extended accordingly.

(6) When* effecting the above mentioned payment ① the Buyer has the right to deduct penalty②, if any③, which may be due to the Seller according to Clause 9 of this Contract.

(7) Payment of expenses due to the seller under Clauses 4.8 and 8.3 of this Contract shall be made in Pounds Sterling to the Seller within 30 days of receipt by the Buyer of Commercial Invoices (5 copies) detailing such charges.

(Excerpts from the Purchase Contract of the China National Machinery Import & Export Corporation.)

---

① 交上述货款 ②扣除罚金 ③如果有的话

CHAPTER THIRTEEN

Inspection

Right of inspection

Careful and proper inspection of commodity[①] is indispensable to ensure that the quality specifications, quantity, packing and packaging of the goods that the buyer wants to purchase, are in conformity with the contract stpulations and the relevant regulations and laws of the state. It is general practice of the exporter to have the goods inspected before shipment, so that he can get the certificates of quality and quantity of the goods and thereby get payment from the negotiating bank. Notwithstanding that, from the legal point of view[②], it is the buyer who should be given the right to inspect the goods he has bought. After all[③], he pays for the goods, so he is entitled[④] to have such a right in the U. S. A. and the U. K, the commercial law stipulates the buyer' s right to inspect the goods at destination or some other place as he chooses, depending upon the delivery terms they agree to.

---

① 商品检验 ②从法律角度 ③毕竟 ④授予

Independent public surveyor

Under either FOB, CFR and CIF delivery terms, the risk of the goods passes from seller to buyer, When the goods have effectively passed over the ship's rail; in other words, for any loss or damage that occurs thereafter, the seller is not held responsible①. In most cases, the buyers inspect the goods after arrval at destination. If loss or damage occurs during transit owing to② some contingency and/or their negligence③, the shippng company and the insurance company should be responsible. As a rule④, a third party is entrusted⑤ with the inspection work, e.g., the China Import and Export Commodity Inspection Bureau in China. It is an official organization ; however, in many foreign countries, an independent public surveyor⑥, a private establishment, is employed to do the work. Apart from⑦ those for which the shipping company or the insurance company is responsible, the certificates of quality and quantity issued by the surveyor serve as evidence for the buyer to lodge a claim for any deficiency⑧ in quality or quantity with the seller. When it is proved that the loss or damage or any deficiency in quality of the goods delivered results from seller's fault⑨, the seller should pay compensation to⑩ the buyer.

---

① 有责任，有义务 ②由于…原因 ③疏忽 ④通常 ⑤委托 ⑥检验员，公证人 ⑦除…以外 ⑧缺陷 ⑨志方的错误 ⑩支付赔偿

When and where to make inspection

The time and place of commodity inspection, the surveyor who is authorized to carry out inspection①, and the method to be used for inspection are the important points in an inspection clause of a sales contract and similarly in a purchase contract. Where and when to perform the right of inspection depends upon different situations. There are three options for the buyer and seller to choose from:

1) When the contract stipulates shipping quality, weight or quantity as final, inspection takes place before shipment and if there are no irregularities② found out at port of shipment, the certificates of inspection issued by the suryeyor, govermmental③ or private, shall be taken as final④. The buyer may reinspect the said goods⑤ at destination; for any deficiency in quality and quantity if it occurs, the buyer cannot hold the seller responsible for that, as the* landing quality and weight do not count⑥.

2) When the contract stipulates the landing quality and weight as final, the goods shall be inspected by a surveyor at destination, whose certificates of inspection shall be regarded as

---

① 进行检验 ②不正常情况，差错 ③政府的 ④作为法律约束 ⑤以上货物 ⑥到岸确定的质量和重量不算数

final. If any deficiency is found, the buyer has the right to file a claim① with the seller.

3) When the contract stipulates that the seller should inspect the goods before shipment and get the relative certificates and the buyer has the right of reinspection at destination. Thus the seller can negotiate with the bank for payment, and the buyer can also get the required certificates②. If there is any difference between the results of those two inspections, none of which is taken as final. They will* hold negotiation to settle the case③. Of course, when the difference is very small, say 0.15% in the case of bulk cargo, both parties would not care to discuss the case any further, considering the difference being* within the range of tolerance④. When the difference is quite appreciable⑤ and no agreement is reached through consultation, they would refer it to arbitration⑥, i. e. , to a third party who is entrusted to make an impartial⑦ inspection, and make a decision to solve the difference.

It is conceivable⑧ that the buyer (consignee) may find it difficult or uneconomical⑨ to perform the inspection at the destination sea port, or, to be exact, at the wharf godown⑩. He-

---

① 提出起诉 ②必需的检验证件 ③进行谈判来解决问题 ④在允许的范围内的，又指免赔额内 ⑤明显的，显而易见的 ⑥仲裁，(指买卖双方达成协议在双方发生争议时，如协商不能解决，自愿将有关争议提交给双方所同意的第三者进行裁决，其结果对双方都有法律约束力) ⑦公平的 ⑧可想象的⑨不合算的 ⑩码头仓库

nce inspection of the imported goods can be made in the factory designated[①] by the buyer, and probably in an inland city, e. g. Sian. Since there is usually a deadline[②] for the buyer to raise any claim, inspection will have to be made within a certain period of time after arrival of the said goods at destination. The length of time allowed depends upon the nature of the goods, i. e. if the goods are liable[③] to deteriorate, inspection must be completed in a relatively short time. At any rate[④], there must be a time limit for the buyer to lodge a claim.

For sophisticated machines, e. g. the generating set. The contract stipulate the techrnical standards and requirements to be used for inspection, e. g. British and Manufacturer′s standards and technical design requirements[⑤], On account of[⑥] their complexity[⑦], they are listed separately[⑧] in an appendix to the sales contract. In certain cases, like sale of aircrafts. the contract stipulates buyer′s undertaking to send a few representatives to the seller′s workshops for scrutiny[⑨] purpose, Who will, under special arrangements, monitor[⑩] the manufacturing process, having access to[⑪] raw materials, blueprints[⑫] and so on in the workshops. Contract provision[⑭] of this kind is necessary for the sake of[⑭] careful inspection as well as quality control. When a complete plant, e. g., a chemical fertilizer plant is bought, inspection has to be made after installation, testrun[⑮]

---

① 指定 ②最后期限 ③容易的 ④无论如何 ⑤技术标准与设计要求 ⑥由于 ⑦复杂性 ⑧分别地 ⑨监督 ⑩跟踪监视 ⑪接近 ⑫蓝图 ⑬条款 ⑭为…起见 ⑮装配与检测

and operation[①] of the said plant at the construction site[②] in China. By that time the buyer or his representative who may be the chief engineer[③] of the plant can be sure of the performance of the complete plant living up to the technical standards laid down[④] in the purchase contract. Furthermore a guarantee period after the plant has been put into operation[⑤] is specified for the buyer to make sure that the plant can* run continuously and smoothly for a period[⑥], say one or two months, without any defect or deficiency revealed. The inspection process lasts much longer than usual in commodity trade.

Inspection clause

Now let us look at the typical inspection clause of China's sales contract (for export goods).

It is mutually[⑦] agree that the certificates of quality and weight issued by the China lmport and Export Commodity Inspection Bureau at the port of shipment shall be part of the documents to be presented for negotiation under the relevant L/C. The Buyers shall have the right to reinspect the quality and weight of the cargo. The reinspection fee[⑧] shall be borne by the Buyers. Should the quality and/or weight be found not

---

① 操作 ②建造工地 ③总工程师 ④规定 ⑤投入使用(运行) ⑥连续不断,毫无故障地运行一段时间 ⑦相互地 ⑧复检费

in conformity with that of the contract, the Buyers are entitled to lodge with the Sellers a claim which should be supported by survey reports① issued by a recognized② surveyor approved③ by the Sellers. The claim, if any, shall be lodged within ... days after arrival of the cargo at the port of destination.

The typical inspection clause of China's purchase contract (for import goods) is as follows:

a. Before making delivery, the manufacturers shall make a precise and comprehensive④ inspection of goods as regards⑤ their quality, specifications, performance and quantity/weight, and issue a certificate certifying that the goods are in conformity with the stipulations of this Contract. The certificate shall form an integral⑥ part of the documents to be presented to the bank for negotiation/collection of payment but shall not be considered as final in respect of⑦ quality, specifications, performance⑧ and quantity/weight of the goods. A written report stating particulars⑨ and results of the test carried out by the manufacturers must be attached to⑩ the quality certificate.

b. After arrival of the goods at the port of destination the Buyers shall apply to the China Import and Export Commodity Inspection Bureau (hereinafter called the Bureau) for inspection

---

① 检验报告 ②信得过的，声誉好的 ③同意 ④准确与全面的 ⑤有关，关于 ⑥完整的 ⑦关于 ⑧性能 ⑨详细情况 ⑩附随

of the goods in respect of their quality, specifications, and quantity/weight if any discrepancies are found by the Bureau regarding the specifications or the quantity/weight or both, except these for which the insurance co. or the shippng co. is responsible, the Buyers shall, within 120 Days after discharge of the goods① at the port of destination, have the right either to reject② the goods and/or to claim against the Sellers on the strength of the inspection certificate issued by the Bureau.

c. Within the guarantee period stipulated in this contract, should the quality and/or the specifications of the goods be found not in conformity with the contracted stipulations, or should the goods prove defective for any reasons, including latent defect③ or the use of unsuitable materials, the Buyers shall arrange for an inspection to be carried out by the Bureau and have the right to claim against the Sellers on the strength of the inspection certificate(s) issued by the Bureau.

d. Any and all claims shall be regarded as accepted if the Sellers fail to reply within 30 days after receipt of the Buyer's claim.

Price adjustment④

It should be mentioned that under certain conditions

---

① 卸货 ②拒收 ③潜在的缺点：指在一般检验中不能发现的缺陷 ④价格调整

depending upon the nature of the commodity, when the quality is found not in conformity with the contracted stipulations, the sellers can get some* pre-determined price reduction① as compensation for inferior② quality instead of rejecting the goods in question③. This adjustment practically constitutes④ part of the price clause.

Examples

(1)

Inspection

If upon receipt of the goods by MACHIMPEX in China, the same shall appear not to conform to the order, or to have shortages⑤, or to be damaged due to improper packing, MACHIMPEX shall within ninety (90) days after arrival of the goods at the port of destination, notify UACL of such conditions and afford UACL a reasonable opportunity to inspect the goods and promptly⑥ make appropriate⑦ adjustment or replacement. The remedies afforded MACHIMPEX under the Article hereof entitled* "Warranties, Remedies and Limitations⑧" shall be exclusively⑨ for defective goods discovered upon inspection, but shall not be cut off⑩ by reason of MACHIMPEX's failure to discover the defective goods within the

---

① 预定价格减去部分 ②低劣的 ③正在谈判 ④组成，构成 ⑤短缺 ⑥马上，立即 ⑦适当的 ⑧担保、补偿、限制 ⑨仅仅 ⑩删去

inspection period provided in this paragragh[1]. MACHIMPEX shall not delay payment for the goods, pending[2] their inspection.

(Excerpts from General Terms of the Agreement between United Aircraft of Canada Limited[3] and the China National Machinery Import & Export Corporation.)

(2)

Weight, Quality and Conditions

Goods shall be weighed, inspected and analysed by the China Import and Export Commodity Inspection Bureau and * Animal and Plant Quarantine Service[4] at the port of destination. Weight specifications and quality conditions as certified by the China Import and Export Commodity Inspection Bureau and Animal Quarantine Service shall be taken as final. The Buyers shall advise by cable discrepancies, if any, within forty days after the date of discharge. The official grade and weight certificates and phytosanitary certificates issued at the loading port(s) are to be used for reference only[5].

Should the specifications and quality conditions of the goods be found materially[6] lower than those stipulated in this Contract, the compensations of quality damage and/or off spec-

---

① 段落 ②在等待期间 ③加拿大联合飞机有限公司 ④动植物检疫服务部 ⑤只作参考 ⑥大大地

ifications[①] must be made by the Sellers to the Buyers based on the Certificates issued by the China Commodity Inspection Bureau and Animal and Plant Quarantine Service. Such compensation of the whole claim is to be paid in full by the Sellers on the FOB value of the goods immediately upon receipt of the relative statements of claims from the Buyers.

--If Foreign Material exceeds[②] 1%, Sellers are to pay 1% of the FOB price for each 1% in excess or pro-rata[③].

--If Test Weight is less than 74,50 kilos/hectolitre[④] at discharge, Sellers are to pay 1% of the FOB price for each 1 kilo deficiency or pro-rata.

--If Moisture exceeds 13.5%. Sellers are to pay 1% of the FOB price for each 1% in excess or pro-rata.

Other claims, if any, in respect of the quality are to be negotiated amicably[⑤] between the Buyers and the Sellers.

As regards weight, the Sellers shall be responsible for any shortage in excess of[⑥] 4% which is not covered by the insurance. Such shortage shall be reimbursed to the Buyers at the Contract price.

(Excerpts from the Contract of the China National Cereals, Oils and Foodstuffs Import and Export Corp.)

---

① 不符合规格 ②超过 ③按比例地 ④百升 ⑤友好地 ⑥超过

(3)

Quality and Weight Inspection

Sellers guarantee that the goods to be delivered shall be of sound quality[①] and fully equal to the sample already in Buyer′s possession. Quality and weight to be certified by an independent public surveyor or the Societe Generale de Surveillane in Assab or Djibouti at time of shipment, fee for seller′s account.

Buyers will re-inspect the goods upon arrival at destination and shall have the right to claim on Sellers if the quality and weight are found not in conformity with certificates. Such claim is to be lodged within 45 days after the arrival of the goods at the port of discharge.

(Excerpts from the confirmation of Ethiopian Commodities P. L. C.)

(4)

Inspection

Prior to the shipment of the goods the inspection shall be carried out by the Sellers and they will issue a certificate of quality and weight. All fees and expenses shall be borne by the Sellers. After the arrival of the goods at the port of destination the Buyers have the right to reinspect. In case the quality and

---

① 完好的质量

quantity of the goods shipped are not in conformity with the contracted stipulations apart from those within the responsibility of shipping company or insurance company ,the Buyers have the right to file a claim against the Sellers within 45 days after discharge of contracted goods.

(Excerpts from the contract signed between Sierra Lione Marketing Board and the China National Native Produce and Animal By-products Import and Export Corporation.)

(5)

Plant Representatives

The Corporation's construction of the Aircraft and all materials and parts obtained by them thereof shall at all reasonable times during business hours be* open to scrutiny① by duly authorized representatives of the Buyer at the Corporation's Works② and if possible at the facilities③ of its respective subcontractors④, and such representatives shall, in order to carry out the aforesaid scrutiny, have access to such relevant technical data as is reasonably necessary for this purpose (except that if access to any part of its works where construction is in process or materials or parts which are stored is restricted⑤ for security reasons the Corporation shall be allowed a reasonable time to make the items available for scrutiny elsewhere.)

---

① 允许监督检查 ②工厂 ③设备 ④分包商 ⑤限制

The actual detailed scrutiny of Aircraft and materials and parts thereof shall only take place in the presence of[①] the Corporation's Inspection Department personnel[②]. For this purpose, and commencing with[③] the date of this Agreement until the delivery of the last Aircraft, the Corporation shall furnish[④], whitout additional charge[⑤], suitable office space and office equipment in or conveniently located near the Corporation's Works for the use of up to but not exceeding four (4) such representatives of the Buyer during the aforementioned period. All scrutiny examinations and discussions with the Corporation's engineering or other personnel by the Buyer's said representatives shall be performed in such manner as not to delay or hinder the manufacture or assembly[⑥] of the Aircraft, or the proper performance of this Agreement by the Corporation.

Inspection and Certification

The Aircraft will be constructed[⑦] in accordance with[⑧] the relevant requirements of the British Government and will be inspected under the Corporation's own system of inspection as approved by the CAA for the British Government and such standards and systems of inspection shall be accepted by the Buyer.

---

① 在场 ②公司检验部门人员 ③从…开始 ④提供 ⑤没有任何附加费 ⑥装配 ⑦装配 ⑧符合

The Corporation shall obtain for each of the Aircraft a British Certificate of Airworthiness① for export in the category②"Transport Category (Passenger)"③

In entering into this Agreement the Corporation is deemed to* have knowledge of all laws and regulations and interpretations thereof④, issued and current at the date hereof, sufficiently to enable the Corporatin to warrant to the Buyer its ability to obtain as hereinbefore provided British Certification of Airworthiness of the Aircraft. If however after the date of this Agreement any new regulation is promulgated⑤ or a new interpretation* comes into operation⑥ before an aircraft is "ready for delivery"(as that expression is defined in Clause 9 of this Agreement) and requires any change to the Specification in order to obtain Certification of Airworthiness of the Aircraft, then the Corporation shall be entitled to make any requisite⑦ or appropriate* variation or modification⑧ to the Specification. In the event⑨ that any such modification or variation should constitute a "major change"⑩ (as that expression is defined in Clause 2 of this Agreement) the parties shall sign an appropriate Alteration Sheet⑪ and the effect (if any) of such modification or variation upon any guarantees or criteria set forth in the Specification

---

① 适航检验证明 ②类别 ③运输类(客运) ④了解全部有关的法律，法规及其细则 ⑤颁布 ⑥实施 ⑦必要的 ⑧变更或修改 ⑨如果 ⑩大的变动 ⑪变更单

and/or upon the date of delivery hereunder of any of the Aircraft affected shall be accepted by the Buyer and the cost of making such modification or variation including the cost of manufacture of additional tools and test equipment shall be borne as to half by the Buyer and as to half by the Corporation. The amount so to be borne by the Buyer shall be added to the basic Contract Price of each of the Aircraft affected by such modification or variation.

Buyer′s Acceptance

1)After the Corporation has conducted its normal production test flight[①] on any of the Aircraft and carried out any corrections necessitated thereby the Acceptance Tests of that Aircraft shall take place at the Corporation′s Works. The tests shall be carried out by personnel of the Corporation(accompanied if the Buyer so wishes by up to three (3)representatives of the Buyer acting as observers[②] and it is the intention[③] of the parties that not later than three (3) months before the first Aircraft is to be ready for delivery a Buyer's Acceptance Schedule[④] will be agreed upon and that compliance with[⑤] such schedule shall then be deemed to demonstrate[⑥] compliance with and functioning in accordance with the Specification. The Corporation shall give to the Buyer not less than six(6)days notice

---

① 测试飞行 ②观察员 ③意向 ④买方检收计划 ⑤一致 ⑥表明

in writing of the proposed time and place[1] of such tests and in the event of the Buyer electing to attend the said Tests he shall co-operate[2] with the reasonable requirements[3] of the Corporation with the intention of completing all Tests within five (5) days after commencement. Failure to attend the Tests or failure so to co-operate shall entitle the Corporation to complete them in the absence of the Buyer who shall be deemed to have accepted the Tests as satisfactory in all respects[4], The Corporation shall not be required in the course of such Acceptance Tests to fly any of the Aircraft for an aggregate period[5] of time in excess of six (6) hours.

2) Should it be established[6] that any of the Aircraft has failed to meet the Specification the Corporation shall without hindrance from the Buyer be entitled to and will carry out any necessary minor[7] changes (or major changes if in this latter case[8] the Buyer approves) and as soon as practicable thereafter the Corporation shall present the said Aircraft for new Acceptance Tests to demonstrate the proper correction of the failure such Tests to be held and carried out in accordance with sub-Clause 8. 1 above.

3) Upon satisfactory completion[9] in respect of any of the Aircraft of the said Acceptance Tests the Buyer shall forthwi-

---

① 提议的时间与地点 ②合作 ③合理的要求 ④在各方面 ⑤总计时间 ⑥规定 ⑦小的，次要的 ⑧后一种情况 ⑨圆满完成

th[1] give to the Corporation in respect of that Aircraft a signed Certificate of Acceptance in triplicate. If the Buyer should fail to give the said Certificate within six(6)days after the completion of such Tests, then the Buyer hereby irrevocably appoints[2] the Corporation its agent to complete and execute[3] the Certificate of Acceptance on the Buyer's behalf.

4) The Corporation shall be entitled without payment or other liability to the Buyer to use the Aircraft prior to their delivery for such flight tests as may be necessary to obtain Type of Airworthiness Certification for the Aircraft and such use shall not prejudice[4] the Buyer's obligation to accept delivery of the Aircraft hereunder.

(Excerpts from the Agreement made by British Aircraft Corporation Limited and CAA.)

(6)

Standards and Inspection

1) The Inspection Standards and Rules are detailed in appendix 5 which forms an integral part of this Contract. The above British and Manufacturers' Standards and the technical design requirements shall form the basis for inspection. The above British Standards shall be supplied by the Seller to the Buyer not later than 2 months prior to the start of delivery of

---

① 即刻 ②指定 ③实施、执行 ④损害

the equipment.

The Seller shall supply to the Buyer the inspection standards and rules for the equipment and materials of the Generation Set within one to two months after the date of signature of the Contract①.

2)For the equipment and materials of the Generation Set supplied under this Contract and delivered by the Seller, the quality control inspection clearance certificate issued by the manufactuer and signed by the Seller shall be taken as the quality certificate of the goods delivered.

3)The Seller shall notify the Buyer of his Plans for assembling, testing and inspection, one month prior to such assembly, tests and inspection on the Contract Generating Set. The Buyer shall have the right to despatch②, at his own expense③, 4-6 Inspectors to witness④ on the spot⑤ the assembling, testing and inspection of the epuipments, and material test certificates. The actual dates of assembling, testing and inspection shall be confirmed by the Seller to the Buyer's representatives 3 days beforehand⑥. Should any equipment or materials fail to meet the stipulations of Clause. 7. 1 regarding quality standards and inspection rules, the Buyer's inspectors have the right to ex-

---

① 签订合同 ②派遣 ③买方自付费用 ④见证 ⑤现场 ⑥提前，事先

press their opinions on such failures. The Seller shall give full regard to① such opinions and take appropriate measures② to ensure the quality of the goods delivered. Any minor discrepancy which does not affect the performance of equipment③ will be corrected in due course during installation at site.

The attendance④ of the Buyer's inspectors at quality and inspection tests shall not diminish⑤ the Seller's obligation as stated in Clause 8 and 9 and Appendix I of this Contract, nor will such attendance be a substitute for the Buyer's inspection at the erection site⑥. The Buyer shall not disassemble⑦ the equipment at site unless inspection reveals⑧ any serious defect. Should the Buyer's inspectors fail to attend the inspections or tests, the manufacturer shall have the right to proceed⑨ with inspections and tests.

4) The technical* documents, drawings, laboratories, tools, apparatus⑩, etc. required by the Buyer's inspectors to carry out their work in accordance with Appendix 5 shall be made available free of charge⑪ by the Seller or the sub-Contractor, and the Seller or the sub-Contractor, shall render⑫ full co-operation and assistance within normal working hours to enable the Buyer's inspectors to perform their tasks.

---

① 非常重视 ②采取适当措施 ③设备的运行 ④出席，到场 ⑤减小 ⑥安装工地 ⑦拆卸 ⑧展示，显示 ⑨继续 ⑩文件、图表、实验室、工具、仪器 ⑪免费 ⑫提供，给予

5) To enable the Buyer properly to carry out erection, maintenance① and operational duties on the Generation Set supplied under this Contract the Buyer reserves the right②, if necessary, at his own expense, to send 4-6 trainees③ to the Seller′s and other appropriate factories in the United Kingdom for training. The Seller′s shall render full co-operation and assistance in this task.

6) The Seller shall be responsible for arranging the relevant visas④ to be provided for the Buyer's inspectors and trainees for their visit to the United Kingdom. The Seller shall render all the other assistance appropriate to* ensure the personal safety⑤, provision of living accommodation⑥, medical care⑦ and reasonable aceess to means of communication⑧ for the Buyer's inspectors and trainees. All expenses of any such visits shall be borne by the Buyer.

7) After arrival of the Generation Set to be supplied under this Contract at the Buyer's construction site, should inspection reveal any shortage in quantity or quality not up to⑨ the stipilations of Clause 7,1, the Buyer shall discuss the matter with the Seller's representative, erection engineer at the site, in the first instance. In case some disputes occur between both sides the

---

① 维修 ②保留权力 ③接受培训的人员 ④签证 ⑤确保人身安全
⑥住宿 ⑦医疗 ⑧通讯工具 ⑨达不到

China Commodity inspection Bureau shall take part in such inspection and will issue an inspection certificate, and this shall be regarded as the basis for the Buyer to ask the Seller to make good any shortages and to replace or repair, as appropriate, defective goods.

(Excerpts from the contract of the China National Technical Import Corp.)

CHAPTER FOURTEEN

Erection Testrun and Operation

Import of complete plant

Before 1980, Chian's technology trade[①] was mainly the import of complete plants[②]. which consisted of both equipment and technology; in other words, both hardware and software[③]. It was then considered unwise to buy equipment alone without the necessary technological knowhow to install and operate the equipment up to the required standards. In order to carry out inspection of the imported equipment satisfactorily to both sides it is necessary to stipulate an additional clause, called "erection, testrun and operation clause." In a sense, this clause is supplementary[④] to the Inspection Clause in a contract for sophisticated machinery, equipment and especially a complete plant. In recent years, the percentage of import of complete plants has decreased, because in 1983 China began to lay emphasis on[⑤] tech-

---

① 技术贸易 ②成套设备 ③硬件与软件 ④补充的 ⑤强调

nical transformation of existing enterprises[①]. Nonetheless[②], it is still worthwhile for us to make a study of this clause, so as to equip[③] ourselves with the basic knowledge about the import of modern equipment and technology. When only technology is involved[④] in a contract, it is entitled technology contract or technological contract in contrast with a contract for commodity trade.

Testrun and operation

Erection, testrun, commissioning[⑤], trial operation and finally putting into operation and production are the technical terms[⑥] used in connection with the inspection and acceptance of a plant. It is somewhat difficult to find the exact Chinese translation for these terms, because different kinds of machinery require a different technique of installation. For instance, take testrun. What do you mean by testrun? Generally speaking[⑦], testrun is arranged in a programme to prove whether the plant can fulfill the technical and economic data of a plant, as stipulated in the contract, depending on the type of machinery that has been contracted for. A power plant[⑧] is different from an ammonia plant[⑨] or a synthetic fibre plant[⑩]. As for a generation set, the testrun may comprise two steps; no load and full

---

① 技术改造现有企业 ②然而 ③使具备 ④只牵涉技术 ⑤试运转 ⑥专业术语 ⑦一般来说 ⑧发电厂 ⑨氨厂 ⑩合成纤维厂

load① test-run. Generally, it is not until the whole process of test-running has proved successful that the plant will be commissioned. Start-up follows commissioning, as in the case of an ammonia plant, or you might call it trial operation. A more advanced test-run, the performance test-run, is to prove the performance successful. Thereafter, the plant will be put into operation. It is hardly possible to standardize these technical terms here in the text. We have to rely upon② the actual practice③ to clarify④ them and give the correct definitions in the contract under the guidance⑤ by those who are competent⑥ both politically and technically.

In the case of a complete plant, inspection at the site of its manufacture is only a preliminary step⑦ which entitles the buyer to ensure the fulfilment of required specifications. This step, although indispensable, does not guarantee that the equipment after installation will operate satisfactorily and be up to the stipulations of the contract. To attain the technical and economic data in full necessitates⑧ a high level of technical knowledge⑨ and assiduous⑩ work on the part of the technical personnel, sometimes requiring the service of foreign technicians. In the contracts, therefore, it must be stipulated that the seller shall

---

① 没有负荷和满负荷 ②依照 ③实际操作 ④区分 ⑤在…指导下 ⑥有资格的，能胜任的 ⑦第一步 ⑧使…成为必要 ⑨高水准的专业知识 ⑩勤奋的

provide all the necessary technical information and blueprints and the number of necessary technicians to take part in the installation. To transform the contract into three steps, namely, assembly and erection, testrun and operation, but it can be more complicated in certain cases.

The responsiblity of the seller does not cease① until such a time when the guarantee period expires after the plant is put into normal operation. The buyer can thus be sure that his requiremets are met. We must guard against* oversight and carelessness②, no matter how slight③, as this might lead to financial loss as well as slowing down industrial production.

EXAMPLES

Erection, Trial Operation, Inspection and Acceptance

1) Erection means the assembly of the equipment and materials supplied by the Seller under this Contract including "full load" and "no load" test running on various parts④.

Test-running covers adjustment⑤ and assembly of the whole equipment system of the Generating Set supplied under this Contract and the preliminary test-running of the complete plant.

Test-running for inspection and acceptance purposes me-

---

① 停止 ②疏忽与粗心 ③小的,微小的 ④对各类部件 ⑤调试

ans formal inspection and acceptance test-running within the period of test-running, in order to prove the various technical and economic data including output①, thermal efficiency②, heat rate as stipulated in Appendix I to this Contract.

Erection, test-running, inspection and acceptance test-running shall all be carried out by the Buyer according to the stipulation of the technical documents supplied by the Seller.

The Buyer shall notify the Seller fourteen (14) days previous to③ erection. If the Seller wishes to send 2-3 representatives to be present during such erection, test-running, inspection and acceptance test-running, the Buyer shall agree to accept the representatives. All licences④, Certificates, Visa and credentials⑤ as may be necessary for the Seller's representatives to travel and perform their duties shall be arranged by the Buyer for the duration⑥ of the erection and testing-period. The expenses of the representatives shall be borne by the Seller.

The Seller's representatives shall express their opinions on the matter regarding the erection, test-running, inspection and acceptance test-running. The Buyer shall give full regard to such opinions.

2)Should there be any damage or defect in the equipment and materials supplied, due to errors in the technical data, docu-

---

① 产出 ②热能效率 ③在…之前 ④许可证 ⑤全权证书 ⑥期间

ments and instructions[1] provided by the Seller, the Seller shall be responsible for replacement, or the Buyer will undertake to have such damage repaired all expenses to be borne by the Seller.

3) Should any damage or defects in the equipment be caused by the failure of the Buyer to carry out erection, test-running, inspection and acceptance test-running according to the technical data, drawings and instructions supplied by the Seller, the Buyer shall be responsible for repair and replacement. The Seller shall replace any such parts as soon as possible with all expenses to be borne by the Buyer.

4) After completion of the erection work of each section, it is neccssary to carry out inspection and adjustment on individual units and the whole system* under dynamic and static conditions[2], including test-running on individual units and combined units, electrical machinery[3], safety equipment, monitor instruments[4] and apparatus, and automatic equipment[5].

When the erection, inspection and test-running of all the equipment is up to the requirements, the test-running on the Generation Set supplied under this Contract may begin.

The test-running of the complete plant shall be operated both with and without load to perform the necessary adjustments and settings[6] and to make the necessary tests including

---

① 说明 ②在运动及静止状态下 ③电动机器 ④监控仪器 ⑤自控设备 ⑥安装

governor test[1], both under static and dynamic conditions, over-speed[2] test, load shedding test[3], alternator voltage regulator[4] test, etc. These tests will be checked to ensure that the guaranteed data stipulated in Appendix I to this Contract is achieved.

5) The test-run for the Generating Set supplied under this Contract shall consist of a performance guarantee test, followed by a full load test of steady and continuous[5] running for 72 hours without interruption[6]. During the first test it is necessary to establish[7] that the whole plant is operating satisfactorily.

If the results of these test-runs are up to the above requirements, then such test-runs shall be regarded as accepted.

If during the course of the above full load test-runs any part of the tests is unsuccessful, it will be necessary to repeat the test-run for the whole plant. The total period for these test-runs of the whole plant shall not exceed 30 days.

6) Should any of the data fail to reach the stipulation of Appendix I to this Contract before the end of the above mentioned test runs, both parties shall agree to settle disputes as follows:

a. If the responsiblity lies with the Seller, the Seller shall pay penalties to the Buyer according to the stipulations of Clause 9 of this Contract.

---

① 控制器 ②超速的 ③(电源过载时)切断某些线路的电源测试 ④发电机电压调节器 ⑤稳定的及连续不断的 ⑥间断 ⑦说明,声明

b. If the responsibility lies with the Buyer, the Buyer shall undertake to settle the matter.

7) If, after 72 hours of test-running, the results are proved to be up to the various data stipulated in Appendix I to this Contract, the Buyer shall issue a certificate showing that acceptance and inspection have been completed and shall send same to the Seller. Thus the inspection and acceptance formalities[①] for the Generation Set supplied under this Contract shall be regarded as finalised.

(Excerpts from the Contract for Gas Turbine Generation Set of the China National Technical Import Corporation.)

Erection, Start-Up Testrun and Acceptance

1) Erection is related to the assembly (assembly, welding[②] and acceptance of the over-sized[③] and overweighted[④] equipment) and erection of the Contract Plant, and shall include such installation, tests, chemical cleaning, catalyst[⑤] loading, equipment checks, and water and steam furnishings[⑥] as are set forth in the relevant technical documents. Start-up[⑦] is related to the introduction[⑧] of natural gas into the process and shall take place after the Buyer has carried out the necessary precommissioning and commissioning activities on the plant after comp-

---

① 手续 ②焊接 ③超大的 ④超重的 ⑤催化剂 ⑥蒸气设备 ⑦启动 ⑧引进，引入

letion of erection. Test-run is related to the test for meeting performance guarantees. Acceptance refers to the fulfillment of performance guarantees on a test-run. In case of failure to meet performance guarantees on a test-run, the site representatives of both parties shall* make investigation and make sure① whose responsibility it is, the Seller's or the Buyer's, for the failure; and take appropriate measures as specified in Paragraph NOs 7 and 8.

2) The erection, start-up and testrun shall be carried out by the Buyer in accordance with the design and the technical instructions of Seller's technicians. The Buyer shall complete the erection work within--months after the effective date of the Contract. Any delay in completion of erection beyond these -- months caused by delay of delivery, repair and replacement of equipment for reasons due to the Seller shall be added to the -- months mentioned in Subsection 11. 2. Should there be any delay in completion of erection beyond these -- months caused by the Buyer the period of -- months specified in Subsection 11. 2 shall not be extended any more.

3) The Buyer shall make available② the personnel for the erection, start-up activities and test-run, as well as the materials specified in Annex No. 4 such as raw materials, water, electricity, steam, compressed air and inert gas③.

---

① 作调查，搞清楚 ②提供 ③压缩空气与情性气体

4) When the Buyer's and Seller's representatives at the site consider that the erection has been completed according to the requirements of the design, they will conduct and take part in those inspections and tests called for by the technical documents and drawings to determine whether the plant has been constructed and erected strictly according to the requirements of the design, technical documents and drawings. If the above has been executed to the satisfaction of both parties, the Certificate of Erection will be signed by the representatives of both parties at the site. At the beginning of erection the Buyer shall advise the Seller in writing of the person who is the authorized representative① sent by the Buyer during the erection, start-up and test-run period of the "Contract Plant".

5) The date for the start-up of the plant after completion of the plant erection shall be agreed upon by the representatives of both parties at the site, but within 15 days after Seller's request for start-up. A period from the signature date of the Certificate of Erection Completion to reaching 80% of design capacity② for 24 consecutive③ hours duration shall be allowed, not to exceed 2 months. From either 2 months after the signature date of the Certificate of Erection Completion or after reaching 80% of design capacity for 24 consecutive hours, whichever is earlier, a period of 4 months shall be allowed during which the

---

① 授权代理 ②能量 ③连续的

performance test-run or runs shall be conducted as provided in Annex 6 and Annex 7. If, however, the performance guarantee test is not successfully fulfilled within the said 4 month period, for reasons due to Seller, then Seller shall be entitled to an extension of one month beyond the 4 month period, with all costs of Seller's technicians during the Additional 1 month period being for Seller's account. The performance guarantees are stipulated in Annex 6. The test-run procedure①, including the length of time for a test-run, is stipulated in Annex 7.

6) If the performance guarantee figure② specified in Annex 6 to the Contract are successfully fulfilled within the period of performance guarantee test, a certificate of Acceptance of the "Contract Plant" shall be signed by both parties with four copies, with two copies each.

7) If, due to the Seller's reasons, the performance guarantee has not been met within the specified testrun period, it can be extended for one month. During this period, the Buyer shall not bear all the costs③ of the Seller's technicians at the site.

If, during such extended one month period performance guarantee still cannot be met, due to Seller's reasons, the site representatives④ of both parties shall determine the penalty amounts⑤ based on the stipulations listed in Annex 6 and 7 and sign the Certificate of Acceptance of the Contract Plant. Buyer

---

① 步骤 ②数据 ③承担所有费用 ④现场代理 ⑤罚金额

shall deduct the amount of penalty, if any, from the payment as stipulated in Subsection[1] 3. 2. 5 B of the Contract.

8) If the test-run cannot be carried out successfully or cannot be carried out at all within six months after the date of completion of erection as referred to in Subsection 10. 2 of this erection owing to reasons caused by the Buyer, the "Contract Plant" shall be deemed as accepted by the Buyer. The Certificate of Acceptance of the Contract Plant shall be signed by both parties.

9) The Acceptance of the plant as provided in Sub-section 10. 6, 10. 7 and 10. 8 of this section shall not free the Seller from the guarantee responsibility for the equipment and materials of the "Contract Plant" within the guarantee period.

(Excerpts from the contract of the China National Technical Import Corporation.)

---

① 小节

CHAPTER FIFTEEN

Force Majeure[1]

Definition of force majeure

What is force majeure? The dictionary defines it as "irresistible force[2]", which is the literal meaning[3] of these French words. It refers to the impediment(s)[4] which is beyond the control of either one of the contracting parties.

Either party could not reasonably be expected to have* taken the impediment into account[5] at the time of the conclusion of the contract or to have avoided or overcome it or its consequence. In other words, only those events which cannot be foreseen, avoided or prevented are classified as force majeure. So far there have been no uniform rules to define exactly what these events are. Generally, they are divdied into two categories:* natural disasters and social causes[6]. Flood, fire, earth quake, thunderbolt[7], storm, hurricane[8], serious drought[9], etc.

---

① 不可抗力 ②不可抵抗的力量 ③文字上的意义 ④意外 ⑤把意外考虑进去 ⑥自然力量与社会力量 ⑦雷电 ⑧飓风 ⑨严重的干旱

are natural calamities[①] owing to act of Gods or what we call natural elements, on which we would not differ from our trade counterparts. However, when force majeure case stems from[②] social cause(s), we might sometimes have different ideas from our trade counterpart, for instance, port congestion[③], raw material shortage, sabotage[④] of transportation agencies, accident in the manufacturing process, epidemics[⑤], strike, lockout[⑥], labour dispute, embargo[⑦] and governmet restriction[⑧]. Do we consider all of them irresistible forces? Some of them are disputable, so we must make concrete[⑨] analysis of the situation to see if it is really beyond human control. We won't agree to port congestion and sabotage of transportation agencies as force majeure. As to riot[⑩], strike and labour dispute[⑪], it is advisable not to list them as force majeure cases. We can discuss and negotiate with our trade counterparts when any one of them should occur, after investigation into the cause and nature of those events.

Force Majeure clause

Thus how to write out the force majeure clause is no easy task and requires serious study. At present, mentioned item by item[⑫] in the contracts are those belonging to the natural irresistible forces, and those problematic[⑬] cases are grouped under

---

① 自然灾害 ②来源于 ③港口拥挤 ④怠工 ⑤流行病 ⑥关闭工厂 ⑦禁运 ⑧政府禁令 ⑨具体的 ⑩暴乱 ⑪工潮 ⑫ 逐款逐款地 ⑬有问题的

the classification as "other cases agreed upon by both parties". It is the accepted wording[1] and serves its purpose for the time being[2], yet it has to be brought up for discussion and revision[3], so that we can arrive at a satisfactory solution from our experience in handling[4] this kind of dispute.

From the examples given hereunder, one can easily understand that there are three approaches[5] to the force majeure clause: (1) a general statement, saying that cases of force majeure will excuse the parties concerned from default[6], (2) enumerate the cases of force majeure item by item in an all-inclusive way[7], (3) enumerate the main cases together with a general supplement, saying: "and others agreed upon by both parties". Probably*, the majority are inclined to adopt the third approach[8]. The reason why the detailed enumeration[9] of the cases of force majeure is inadvisable[10] seems quite simple; every now and then[11] a new case of force majeure appears and, therefore, one cannot make out a complete list of all the force majeure cases. For instance, take the energy crisis[12]. It started in 1973 and has continued to be a* thorny problem[13] for many years. We should not recognize it as a case of force majeure. Maybe, some other new cases would arise next year. For this reason, it is preferable to mention such force majeure cases as

---

① 措辞 ②暂时 ③修改 ④处理、解决 ⑤方法 ⑥违约 ⑦以包含切的方式 ⑧绝大部分趋向于采取第三种方式 ⑨详细例举 ⑩ 不可取的 ⑪常常 ⑫能源危机 ⑬棘手的问题

we recognize and admit of no argument. At the same time, we leave the clause open for other possible cases. We may tackle① those not enumerated in contracts, when they are brought up by the overseas merchants, and consult with② each other to reach any agreement. This way is flexible and acceptable to both parties.

Part One

1) Force Majeure

The Sellers shall not be held responsible for the delay in shipment or non-delivery of the goods due to Force Majeure, which might occur during the process of manufacturing or in the course of loading or transit. The Sellers shall advise the Buyers immediately of such occurrence③ and within fourteen days thereafter, the Sellers shall send by airmail to the Buyers for their acceptance a certificate issued by the competent Government Authorities where the accident occurs as evidence thereof. Under such circumstances the Sellers, however, are still under obligation to take all necessary measures to hasten④ the delivery of the goods. In case the accident lasts for more than ten weeks the Buyers shall have the right to cancel⑤ the Contract.

---

① 处理 ②协商 ③发生,事件 ④加速 ⑤取消

(Excerpts from the contract of the China National Machinery Import and Export Corporation.)

2) In case of Force Majeure the Sellers shall not be held responsible for delay in delivery or non-delivery of the goods but shall notify immediately the Buyers by cable and deliver to the Buyers by registered mail① a certificate issued by government authorities or Chamber of Commerce② as evidence thereof. If the Force Majeure lasts over one month the Buyers shall have the right to cancel this Contract. Seller's liability to obtain export licence shall not be considered as Force Majeure. (Excerpts from the Contract of the China National Metals & Minerals Import and Export Corp.)

Part Two

Should the shipment within the stipulated period be prevented by Act of God, strikes, lockouts, labour disturbances, trade disputes, war, government action, riots, civil commotions③, fires, floods or epidemics, the time of shipment shall be extended for six weeks after which this Contract shall be* null and void④ for any portion which shall not have been executed at that time unless a further extension is granted by mutual agreement.

---

① 挂号邮寄 ②商会 ③民变 ④无效,作废

If either party intends to claim protection of this Clause he must give reasonably prompt notification[①] and, if required, furnish proof[②] to justify his claim[③]. (Excerpts from International CIF C&F FOB Contracts No. 15, January, 1973.)

Part Three

(1)

The Sellers shall not be held responsible for the delay in shipment or non-delivery of the products due to Force Majeure of serious natural disaster, lock-out and war, which might occur during the process of manufacturing or in the course of loading or transit. The Sellers shall advise the Buyers immediately of the occurrence mentioned above and within fourteen days thereafter, the Sellers shall send by airmail to the Buyers for their acceptance a certificate of the accident issued by the Government Authorities where the accident occurs as evidence thereof. Under such circumstances the Sellers, however, are still under obligation to take all necessary measures to hasten the delivery of the products.

In case the accident lasts for more than three months the Buyers shall have the right to cancel the part of delayed delivery.

(Excerpts from the contract of the China National Machinery Import and Export Corporation.)

① 立刻通知 ②提供证据 ③为…起诉辩护

(2)

FORCE MAJEURE

1. Should either of the Parties to the Contract be prevented from performing their obligations[①] under the Contract by such cases of Force Majeure as war, fire, floods, earthquake, and other cases agreed upon by both parties, the time for performance of those obligations shall be extended by a period equal to the effect of those cases.

2. The prevented Party shall notify by cable the other Party within the shortest possible time of the occurrence of the force majeure and airmail to the other Party for its confirmation within 14 days thereafter a certificate issued by the competent authorities.

3. Should the effects of Force Majeure continue more than 120 days both parties shall settle the further execution[②] of the Contract through friendly negotiations as soon as possible.

(Excerpts from the contract of the China National Technical Import Corp.)

---

① 履行义务 ②实施

CHAPTER SIXTEEN

Warranty and Remedy

Warranty Clause①

"Warranty" is a commercial term used in a business contract. Guaranty is sometimes interchangeable② with warranty. However, guaranty may be offered by a third party③ to the buyer, while warranty is used between the buyer and the seller only. Remedy, correction or indemnity④ is given or made when the seller is held responsible for a defect or defects of a machine or similar product and has to compensate the buyer for the loss or damage. Correction means to correct the defect. When payment is involved, the remedy is an indemnity.

Under the warranty clause, the seller's liabilities should be defined, so that both parties will know what to do and how, in case of something unforeseen happening during the execution of the contract. If the goods are found in conformity with the contract stipulations in every detail and everything else turns

---

① 保证条款 ②可互换的 ③第三方 ④赔偿，补偿

out satisfactory, no one would care to trouble the other party. If the quality of the goods, after proper inspection, is found inferior to that of the contract stipulation, the buyer has the right to take recourse to the seller, after ascertaining[①] how the quality discrepancy has come about. If the deterioration of quality has occurred during the transit, then the insurance company is responsible for it, provided the risk has been covered in an insurance policy[②]. If , however, the goods are shortlanded[③], the steamship company[④] should be approached for the settlement of the claim. If a machine is found defective at delivery, either as a result of faulty material, poor workmanship or faulty design, it is the seller who is responsible and the buyer is entitled to file a claim with the seller. A case like this requires a technical analysis. If there is a minor defect, which can be easily corrected by the buyer, he can get permission[⑤] from the seller who will bear the cost of such a correction.

How to make remedy

Sometimes, one or two parts of a machine are defective consequently, its normal operation is affected. In such a case, there are three possible solutions[⑥].

1)The seller replaces the defective part or parts.

2)The buyer repairs the defective part or parts at the seller's expense.

---

① 确定 ②保险单 ③短卸 ④轮船公司 ⑤许可 ⑥解决办法

3) The seller replaces the whole machine, which is possible only if the damage is beyond repair or the machine cannot be restored① to the operating level as stipulated in the contract. The solution depends upon the actual conditions of the defects.

Any way the warranty clause stipulates that the seller shall be under obligation to take prompt action to correct the defects, or else he is in default and, therefore, subject to legal action②. That would also be undesirable from the seller's standpoint③ as it is a matter of maintaining his commercial reputation④. In this sense, the warranty clause affords protection to the buyer.

Need for limitations

The warranty and remedy clause sets the limit to the seller's liabilities ---- what we call "limitations". In this sense, it protects the interests of the seller. For instance, in case when the seller fails to deliver the machine at the time stipulated in the contract, and such delay affects the construction of a whole plant and* brings about financial loss⑤ to the buyer. If the delay is entirely due to the seller's fault, the seller shall pay a penalty to the buyer to compensate him for the loss. On the other hand, the same clause also stipulates the maximum penal-

① 恢复 ②法律手段 ③立场 ④维护商业信誉 ⑤带来经济损失

ty to be paid to the buyer, say, five or ten percent of the total contract price as the case may be. The buyer, in order to protect his interests, reserves the right to cancel the contract, if the time for replacing or repairing the defective machines exceeds seven months or a period of time agreed upon by both parties. One can see that warranty and remedy (or warranty and indemnity) are the two aspects of the same problem, which both parties should take into serious consideration. In any case, both the buyer and the seller shall hold mutual consultation to settle the problem when it arises; or submit it to arbitration①.

Resort to litigation②

"Tort③" is a civil wrong inflicted④ otherwise than by a breach of contract. Elements of a tort are (1) a wrongful act⑤ or* omission to obey the law⑥, and (2) an injury to some person. Tort gives the injured party the right to sue for⑦ any resulting financial loss. Sometimes a claim for compensation is filed against the seller owing to damage to property⑧ or bodily injury in cases which the sales contract has not dealt with⑨. It is not a violation⑩ or contract stipulation. Then the injured party may make an appeal⑪ to law court⑫, instead of arbitration, adjudication⑬ will be made according to the Civil Code i. e. ,

---

① 递交仲裁 ②求助法律诉讼 ③民事侵权行为 ④使遭受 ⑤非法行为 ⑥没有守法 ⑦提出诉讼 ⑧财产 ⑨涉及 ⑩破坏 ⑪上诉 ⑫法庭 (13)裁决

tort of the country[①]. In such a case, litigation may bring about a possible solution.

Penalty

Breach of contract entitles the buyer to claim damages from the seller. It is compensative in nature, as the compensation the injured party[②] receives is to cover the losses incurred. However, the damges may include penalty in certain cases, such as late delivery on the part of the seller and delayed establishment of letter of credit on the part of the buyer. In the contracts, the scope of application[③] and the amount of penalty should be clearly defined, so that there will not be any trouble in case penalty is demanded, under the civil law system, by the injured party. Generally, the seller is not held responsible for payment of any indirect or consequential loss or damage, nor is he subject to penalty for such loss or damage ---- a stipulation which both parties will adhere to[④]. We must be clear what losses or damages should be considered to be consequential loss or damage.

It is noteworthy[⑤] that the Convention[⑥] does not mention penalty, presumably[⑦] because imposition of penalty is not legally permissible[⑧] under the common law system. Thus the term

---

① 《民事法》 ②受害方 ③应用范围 ④遵守 ⑤值得指出的 ⑥惯例 ⑦大概 ⑧允许

"damages" is more acceptable worldwide than penalty. When we draft the stipulation of penalty in international sales contract, we must take into consideration the law of the state with which we are dealing in respect of penalty.

Patent right

Nowadays, a more complicated problem is about the patent right. The warranty clause stipulates that the seller shall be held responsible for any infringement on the patent right of the equipment as supplied per contract, or the process of manufacturing and putting the equipment into operation. In this way, the buyer is protected from legal entanglement① for the use of the equipment. At the same time, it stipulates that the buyer shall not disclose② to a third party the proprietary technique③ and technical knowhow. The seller must make sure that his patent right is protected.

Therefore, we should be certain as to the requirements laid down in a contract concerning warranty in connection with④ patent right, otherwise a warranty might turn out to be an empty promise⑤.

In international trade, the owner of a patent right may grant a licence⑥ to a company in a foreign country to manufac-

---

① 纠缠,麻烦 ②泄露 ③业主私有技术 ④与…有关 ⑤许诺落空,空话 ⑥颁发许可证

ture machines or other goods of special design. In this sense, "licence" means a permission to use someone else's patent right; this is not an infringement[①]. The licencee[②] can buy the licence from the foreign manufacturer for a lumpsum[③] or agree a yearly payment (royalty) based on the sales amount of the particular product. In such a case, a licensing agreement must be signed between the licensee and the licensor[④]. Since it is simply a case of technical transfer[⑤], the contract in this connection is called technology or technological contract, which is not discussed in this book. Technology trade is considered to be a special branch of international business.

Examples

(1)

Guarantee of quality

The sellers guarantee that the commodity hereof is made of the best materials with first class workmanship[⑥], brand new[⑦] and unused, and complies in all respects with the quality and specification stipulated in this Contract.

Claims[⑨]

Within 90 days after the arrival of the goods at destination, should the quality, specification, or quantity be found not

---

① 侵权人 ②许可证承领人 ③一次性总金额 ④使用费;如版费 ⑤让人使用许可证者 ⑥技术转让 ⑦一流的做工 ⑧全新 ⑨索赔:一方根据其声称的合法权利向另一方提出的赔偿要求

in conformity with the stipulation of the contract except those claims for which the insurance company or the* owners of the vessel① are liable, the buyers shall, on the strength of the Inspection Certificate issued by the China Import and Export Commodity Inspection Bureau, have the right to claim for replacement of new goods, or for compensation, and all expenses (such as inspection charges②, freight for returning the goods and for sending the replacement, insurance premium, storage and loading and unloading charges, etc.) shall be borne by the sellers.

The Certificate so issued③ shall be accepted as the base of a claim. The sellers, in accordance with the buyer's claim, shall be responsible for the immediate elimination④ of the defects, complete and partial replacement of the commodity or shall devalue⑤ the commodity according to the state of defects. Where necessary, the buyers shall be at liberty⑥ to eliminate the defects themselves at the sellers' expense. If the sellers fail to answer the buyers within one month after the receipt of the claim aforesaid, the claim shall be reckoned as⑦ having been accepted by the sellers.

(Excerpts from the contract of the China National Light Industrial Products Import and Export Corporation.)

---

① 船东 ②商检费 ③签发 ④排除 ⑤贬值，降低…的价格 ⑥有权 ⑦把…的看作

(2)

Quality/quantity discrepancy and claim

In case the quality and/or quantity/weight are found by the buyers to be not in conformity with the Contract after arrival of the goods at the port of destination, the buyers may lodge a claim with the sellers supported by survey report issued by an inspection organization agreed upon by both parties, with the exception,① however, of those claims for which the insurance company and/or the shipping company are to be held responsible. Claim for quality discrepancy should be filed by the buyers within 30 days after arrival of the goods at the port of destination, while for quantity/weight discrepancy claim should be filed by the buyers within 15 days after arrival of the goods at the port of destination, The sellers shall, within 30 days after receipt of the notification of the claim, send reply to the buyers.

(Excerpts from the contract of the China National Metals & Minerals lmport and Export Corporation.)

(3)

Guarantee, indemnities and penalty

1) The seller guarantees that the designs and technology of the contract plant shall be the most up-to-date② and the most sophisticated③ among the plants of similar type exported by the

---

① 除外 ②现代的 ③先进的

seller at the time of the effective date of this Contract, and that the contents are complete and correct, and that the equipment and materials are of correct types and fabrication, ① of first grade quality and in conformity with the process of the Contract plant and the requirements for long term operation. Performance guarantees are specified in Annex 6 to this Contract.

2) The guarantee period of the equipment and material supplied under this Contract shall be 12 months from the date when the plant has operated at 80% of design capacity for 24 consecutive hours, and/or 14 months from the date of completion of erection and/or 48 months from the effective date② of the Contract, whichever comes first.

3) If the equipment and material are found defective within the guarantee period, the seller must check the causes of the above mentioned defects together with the buyer as soon as possible after receiving the written notification③ from the buyer. If the seller is found responsible, he shall correct the defects or replace the equipment and material, and the expenses shall be borne by the seller in accordance with the present Contract. In accordance with the guarantee period as specified in Subsection 11.2, the guarantee period of the new replacement of equipment and material extends over 12 months.

---

① 装配、制作 ②有效日 ③书面通知

4)If smaller defects are found on equipment and/or material during the guarantee period, the buyer shall notify the seller, and with the agreement of the seller, the buyer shall correct the defects, and the expense shall be borne by the seller.

5)In case the equipment and material have not been delivered according to the delivery terms laid down in section 5, the seller shall pay the buyer a penalty as follows:

For 0-2 weeks, there shall be no penalty.

For 3-4 weeks the seller shall pay the buyer a penalty equivalent to 0.25% of the value of the delayed equipment and materials for each week's delay.

For 5-8 weeks the seller shall pay the buyer a penalty equivalent to 0.5% of the value of the delayed equipment and materials for each week's delay.

For 9 weeks and over the seller shall pay the buyer a penalty equivalent to 1.0% of the value of the delayed equipment and materials for each week's delay.

The payment of the penalty shall not release the seller from the obligation of delivery.

If due to seller's failure[①] the shipment of equipment and materials has been delayed for over 7 months, the buyer has the right to cancel the present contract partially or complete-

---

① 错误,失败

ly,[①] and claims shall be made against the seller for the refund[②] of advance payment plus interest[③] from the date of advance payment to the date of refunding. Both parties should hold an amicable consultation[④] to find the solution to the problem and reach an agreement[⑤] before the cancellation is made by the buyer.

6) If the designs and technical documentation[⑥] have not been delivered according to the delivery terms and schedules[⑦] of Annex 4 to the contract, and the delay is attributable to[⑧] the fault of the seller, then the seller shall be responsible for any delays in the performance of buyer′s work actually caused by such late delivery. Also, the period of the mechanical guarantees[⑨] shall be extended if appropriate.

7) In case the capacity, product quality and consumption figures as specified in Annex 6 to the contract are not fulfilled during the test-run, due to the seller′s error, the seller shall pay the buyer the amount of penalty in accordance with Annex 7 to the contract.

8) Seller′s total liability for the penalties stipulated in Subsection 11.5 and 11.7 shall not exceed 5% of the total contract price. Seller′s total liability for all obligations assumed[⑩] under

---

① 部分或全部取消合同 ②偿还 ③加上利息 ④进行友好协商 ⑤达成协议 ⑥文件 ⑦规定时间 ⑧归因于…… ⑨机械的保证 ⑩承担

this Contract, exclusive of the obligations assumed by the Sellers under Subsection 4. 1 and 11. 9, shall not exceed 10% of the total Contract price.

9) Until plant acceptance, the seller shall indemnify and keep indemnified the buyer against all direct losses for damage to any of the buyer's property forming part of the seller's supply and caused by the seller's faulty design, faulty equipment and/or faulty instructions. The seller shall be released from his obligations in case the seller's specialists① are not allowed to go to the plant site.

The buyer and the seller shall bear all losses due to property damage or bodily injury② to their own personnel. Eventual amounts③ to be paid under this Subclause are independent from these mentioned in Subclause 11. 8.

10) The time for repairing or replacing equipment caused through the seller's fault is limited to a maximum of 7 months. After 7 months, it is necessary for both parties to hold negotiations for solving the problem. The buyer, at the request of④ the seller, may correct the small defects, if possible at the plant site. The actual expenses arising therefrom shall be borne by the seller.

In the event that the equipment the material and the tec-

---

① 专家 ②身体受伤 ③最后的总额 ④出于…要求

hnical documents get lost or damaged due to the buyer′s error, the seller shall replace same in due time at the buyer′s expense. If the buyer asks for a modification of the design, the seller shall carry out the modification immediately both parties have agreed on price, delivery time, related guarantees as well as on the execution of the work for the "Contract Plant".

(Excerpts from the contract for ammonia plant of the China National Technical Import Corp.)

(4)

Warranties, Remedies & Limitations

1. Defective Goods

UACL warrants to MACHIMPEX that at the time of delivery the goods sold hereunder① will be free from defects in manufacture and material and will conform substantially② to UACL′s applicable③ specifications as stipulated in this agreement. UACL′s liability and MACHIMPEX′S remedy under this warranty are limited to the repair or replacement at UACL′s election of goods④ or parts thereof returned to UACL which are shown to UACL′S reasonable satisfaction to have been defective; provided that written notice of the defect shall have been given by MACHIMPEX to UACL within ninety

---

① 以下 ②主要地,完全地 ③可适应的 ④选货

(90) days or one hundred fifty (150) flying hours, whichever first occurs after acceptance of such aircraft by its first operator[①] but in no event later than one (1) year after the date of delivery of such goods by UACL. Transportation charges[②] for the return of defective goods to UACL and their reshipment to MACHIMPEX and the risk of loss thereof will be borne by UACL only if returned goods[③] are shipped in accordance with written shipping instructions from UACL.

2. Title

UACL warrants to MACHIMPEX that it will convey good title to the goods hereunder. UACL'S liability and MACHIMPEX's remedy under this warranty are limited to removal[④] of any title defect or, at the election of UACL, to the replacement of the goods or parts thereof which are defective in title: provided, however, that the rights and remedies of the parties with respect to patent infringement shall be limited to the provision in paragraph 3, below.

3. Patent Infringement.[⑤]

UACL shall* conduct, at its own expenses the entire defense of any claim[⑥], suit or action[⑦] alleging[⑧] that, without further combination, the use or resale by MACHIMPEX or any

---

① 操作员 ②运费 ③退货 ④排除 ⑤专利侵权 ⑥对索赔全面保护 ⑦起诉或诉讼 ⑧声称

subsequent purchaser or user① of the goods delivered hereunder directly infringes any United States patent or Canadian patent, but only on the conditions that (a) UACL receives prompt written notice of such claim, suit or action and full opportunity and authority to assume the sole defense② thereof, including settlement and appeals③, and be given all information available to MACHIMPEX and defendant④ for such defense; and (b) said goods are made according to specification or design furnished by UACL or, if a process patent is involved, the process performed by the goods is recommended in writing by UACL; and (C) the claim, suit and action is brought against MACHIMPEX or one expressly indemnified by MACHIMPEX, provided all of the foregoing conditions have been met, UACL shall, at its own expense, either settle said claim, suit or action or shall pay all damages excluding consequential damages⑤ and costs awarded by the court therein, and if the use or resale of such goods is finally enjoined⑥, UALC, shall, at UACL′s option⑦, (Ⅰ)procure for⑧ defendant the right to use or resell the goods, (Ⅱ)replace them with equivalent non-infringing goods, (Ⅲ)modify them so they become non-infringing but equivalent, or (Ⅳ)remove them and refund the pur-

---

① 购买者 ②单独提出辩护 ③诉讼 ④被告 ⑤事后带来的损坏 ⑥禁止 ⑦由…选择 ⑧努力争得

chase price (less a reasonable allowance[①] for use, damage and obsolescence[②]). If a claim, suit or action is based on design or specification furnished by AMCHIMPEX or on the performance of a process not recommended in writing by UACL or on the use or sale of the goods delivered hereunder in combination with other goods not delivered to MACHIMPEX by UACL, MACHIMPEX shall indemnify and save UACL harmless therefrom.

4. Exclusive Warranties and Remedies

The foregoing warranties are exclusive and are given and accepted in lieu of[③] (I)any and all other warranties, express or implied[④] including without limitation the implied warranties of merchant ability and fitness for a particular purpose; and (Ⅱ) any obligation, liability, right, claim or remedy in contract or tort, whether or not arising from UACL'S negligence, actual or imputed. The remedies of MACHIMPEX shall be limited to those provided herein to the exclusion of any and all other remedies including, without limitation, incidental[⑤] or consequential damages. No agreement varying or extending the foregoing warranties, remedies or this limitation will be binding upon[⑥] UACL unless in writing signed by a duly authorized officer of UACL.

① 减价 ②陈旧 ③作…的替代 ④不明示的 ⑤意外的 ⑥约束

5. Liability Limitation

The price allocable[①] in this contract to any product or service alleged to be the cause of any loss or damage to MACHIMPEX shall be the ceiling limit[②] on UACL′s liability whether founded in contract or tort (including negligence), arising out of, or resulting from[③] (Ⅰ) this contract or the performance or breach thereof, (Ⅱ) the design, manufacture, delivery, sale, repair, replacement or (Ⅲ) the use of any such product or the furnishing of any such service. In no event shall UACL have any liability for any incidental or consequential damages.

(Excerpts from the general terms agreement between the China National Machinery Import and Export Corp. and United Aircraft of Canada Limited.)

(5)

License and Confidentiality[④]

1) The buyer shall be liable neither at law whatsoever nor in the economic field[⑤], but the seller shall be liable for infringing the patents of the third party in respect of the equipment, process, production method and proprietary techniques.

2) Without the seller′s written consent[⑥], the buyer shall not disclose to third parties the construction design, drawings

---

① 分给，规定 ②最高限价 ③起因于 ④保密性 ⑤经济领域 ⑥书面承诺

and other information of the ammonia plant; and technical data and documentation supplied by the buyer shall not be disclosed by the seller to third parties either.

3) The buyer shall not expand the plants by the same process without the seller's written consent. But, if the capacity of the plant is increased by the buyer by means of[①] improvement of the production or debottle-necking[②] of the plant, the buyer need not ask for the seller's consent, nor pay anything to the seller.

(Excerpts from the contract for ammonia plant)

① 用…方法 ②解决瓶颈

CHAPTER SEVENTEEN

Arbitration, Taxes and Other Provisions

Significance of Arbitration[1]

Arbitration is a means of settling a dispute between two parties through the medium[2] of a third party who is not partial[3] to either of the parties to the dispute, and whose decision on the dispute is final and binding. Mediation or conciliation[4] is to help the parties in dispute to arrive at an equitable[5] solution themselves. The conciliator gets the parties together, makes the arrangement for a meeting and tries to prevent friction[6]. The mediator, however, takes a more positive part[7] in settling the dispute. He proposes solutions that are acceptable to both parties. Frequently, either one performs the function of both.

When disputes arise in foreign trade matters, we try to settle them through friendly negotiation or friendly consultat-

---

① 仲裁的意义 ②方式 ③不公平的 ④调解或调和 ⑤公正的 ⑥摩擦，纠纷 ⑦起积极作用

ion. In fact, the majority of such cases are settled in this manner. We have taken this kind of approach ever since liberation and it is appreciated by our business friends abroad. We should however, stipulate in the contracts an arbitration clause, because there are cases now and then which call for arbitration.

Place of arbitration

Sometimes the cases of dispute are submitted to①* the Foreign Economic and Trade Arbitration Commisson of the China Council for Promotion of International Trade②, Beijing, in accordance with the Provisional Rules of Procedure③ of the above-mentioned commission. As the said Commission has a good reputation in business circles④ the world over, it was once the established practice⑤ that arbitration took place in China in the early 1950′s. However, as our foreign trade is at present developing rapidly and extensively⑥, we may accept arbitration in the defendant′s country, or in Sweden or other countries. The place of arbitration is very important as this decides which procedure be adopted and which arbitration act observed⑦.

A flexible⑧ approach is desirable. In export business, we prefer arbitration in China or in the defendant′s country, while

---

① 提交 ②中国贸易促进会对外经济贸易仲裁委员会 ③暂行的程序规定 ④商业界 ⑤惯例 ⑥广泛地 ⑦遵循何种仲裁法 ⑧灵活的

in import business, in the plaintiff's country[①]. In view of the increase in foreign trade, it is our duty to study arbitration act and other related matters, so that we may know how to defend our interests when* driving a bargain[②] with our trade counterpart abroad.

Taxes, duties[③] and other levies[④] vary in different countries. It is recommended that in our import and export trade we stipulate taxes, duties and other levies outside China be for the account of foreign businessmen; those incurred in China are for our account. This is simple and clear, and usually acceptable to both parties.

Under the heading of "Contract Effectiveness", some legal technicalities[⑤] ought to be clarified, so that there will be no misunderstanding[⑥] about details, such as how to deal with the assignment[⑦] of any obligation and how to construe[⑧] and interpret clauses in a contract. For instance, we must know what to do and say, when the foreign businessmen insist on interpretation of contract stipulations according to the rules and regulations of their country.

Be prudent

In conclusion, it must be stressed that a good contract is

---

① 原告 ②讨价还价 ③税 ④收费 ⑤技术细节 ⑥误解 ⑦转让 ⑧解释

an organic entity[1], and, therefore, should be consistent, as far as the contract stipulations are concerned. If you discover contradictions[2] within a contract, they must be corrected. Any oversight or omission to insert[3] any necessary stipulations will surely lead to disputes and bring about financial as well as political adverse effects[4].

Bargaining preceding the signing of a contract is often sharp. The drawing up of a contract revolves upon[5] business negotiations which are the foundation for making a contract. A successful contract depends primarily upon successful business negotiation on our part . It would be inexcusable[6], if we should miss any advantages that can be gained at the conference table[7]. Above all[8], as a matter of principle, no violation of our government policy of foreign trade should be tolerated in our contract stipulations.

Examples

(1)

Arbitration

All disputes in connection with the execution of this contract shall be settled through friendly negotiations, failing which, each party shall appoint one arbitrator[9] who will nominate[10] one umpire[11] thus to form an arbitration committee. Ar-

---

① 有机统一体 ②矛盾 ③插入 ④不利的,有害的 ⑤围绕着 ⑥不可原谅的 ⑦谈判桌 ⑧总之 ⑨仲裁员 ⑩指定 ⑪首席仲裁员

bitration is to take place at ----. The award[①] of the Arbitration Committee shall be accepted as final by both parties for settlement. Arbitration fee, unless otherwise awarded, shall be borne by the losing party[②]. The Arbitrators and the umpire shall be confined to persons of Chinese or ---- Nationality.

In case the Arbitration is to be held in Beijing, the case in dispute shall be then submitted to the Foreign Economic and Trade Arbitration Commission of the China Council for the Promotion of International Trade, Beijing, in accordance with the Provisional Rules of Procedure of the said Arbitration Commission. The decision by the Commission shall be accepted as final and binding upon both parties.

(Excerpts From the Contract of the China National Light Industrial Products Improt & Export Corporation.)

(2)

Arbitration

In case of any dispute arising in the course of execution of this Contract or growing out of this Contract, the two contracting parties shall first reach a settlement by way of amicable negotiation, failing which they may have recourse to arbitration. The arbitration shall take place where the defendant resides[③]. Each party shall appoint one arbitrator and the arbitrators of both parties shall select a third party as chief arbitrator[④] to proceed with[⑤] the arbitration. The decision of their arbitr-

① 裁决 ②败诉方 ③居住 ④首席仲裁员 ⑤进行

ation shall be final and binding upon both parties. The arbitration expenses, unless it is awarded otherwise, shall be paid by the party who has lost the case.

(Excerpts from the contract signed between Sierra Leone Marketing Board and the China National Native Produce and Animal By-products Import & Export Corporation.)

(3)

Arbitration

1) All disputes[1] between the Parties arising from this Contract shall be settled by friendly consultations between parties.

In case where no settlement can be reached through consultation, such dispute shall be submitted to arbitration.

2) The place of arbitration shall be (Stockholm, Sweden) and the arbitration shall be carried out according to Swedish Arbitration Procedures[2].

3) The Arbitration Committee shall consist of one representative appointed by each party to act for it and another Swedish member agreed upon by both parties. The decision of the Arbitration shall be binding on both parties and parties shall act accordingly.

4) The relative arbitration fee shall be borne by the Party adjudicated against.

---

① 争议 ②瑞典仲裁程序

(Excerpts from the Contract signed with Brown Engineering Co. Ltd.)

(4)

Arbitration

All disputes in connection with the execution of this contract shall be settled friendly through negotiations. Should no settlement ① be reached, the disputes shall be submitted for arbitration.

Each party shall appoint an arbitrator within thirty 30 days after receipt of notification from the opposite party②, and the two arbitrators thus appointed shall jointly③ nominate a third person of Swedish nationality as umpire to form an arbitration Committee.

The Arbitrators shall be confined④ to citizens of Chinese or French nationality. The Arbitration Committee shall render a fair judgement.

The decision given by the Arbitration Committee shall be final and binding upon both parties; neither parties shall seek recourse to a law court or other authorities to appeal for revision of the decision.

The Arbitration expenses shall be borne by the losing party.

---

① 解决 ②对方 ③共同地 ④限制

The Arbitration shall take place in STOKHOLM with reference to the Swedish Arbitration Law.

(Excerpts from the contract with the Societe National Inductrielle Aeros Spatiale, Paris, France.)

(5)

Arbitration

1) All disputes in connection with this Contract shall be settled by friendly consultation between both parties. In case no agreement can be reached, disputes shall be submitted to arbitration.

2) The place of arbitration is Stockholm, Sweden and the arbitration shall be conducted in accordance with Swedish arbitration procedures.

3) An arbitration committee consisting of 3 (three) persons will be formed by 1 (one) each from both the Buyer and the Seller and another member of Swedish nationality, to be agreed upon by both parties.

4) The award given by the said committee shall be regarded by both parties as final and binding ①. An arbitration award in favour of② either party shall be negotiable for payment instead of any other documents in accordance with the stipulations in Section 3 of the Contract.

---

① 有法律作用，对双方都有约束力 ②对…有利

5) The costs of arbitration shall be borne by the losing party unless otherwise decided by the said committee.

6) Performance of the present Contract shall continue during arbitration.

(Excerpts from the Contract of the China National Technical Import Corp.)

Taxes (1)

1) All taxes, customs [①] and other duties in connection with the performance of this Contract arising before the goods are effectively loaded on board the carrying vessel[②], shall be borne by the Seller.

2) All other taxes, customs and duties in connection with the performance of this Contract arising after the goods are effectively loaded on board the carrying vessel, shall be borne by the Buyer.

(Excerpts from the contract of the China National Machinery Import & Export Corp.)

Taxes (2)

In addition to the agreed purchase price of the goods, any and all taxes, rates, duties, imposts and excise charges[③] (not including any income or excess profit taxes[④]) which may be held responsible for collection or payment either on its own behalf[⑤]

---

① 关税 ②运载船只 ③征(税等)与货物税 ④收入所得税与超额利润税 ⑤代表自己

or that of MACHIMPEX shall be paid by MACHIMPEX to UACL upon UACL's demand.

(Excerpts from the General Terms Agreement between United Aircraft of Canada Limited and China National Machinery Import and Export Corp.)

Taxes and Duties (3)

1) Taxes: All taxes incurred in Japan in connection with this Contract, shall be borne by the Builder and all incurred elsewhere shall be borne by the Buyer.

2) Duties: The Builder shall hold the Buyer harmless of and from any payment of any import duties imposed by Japan upon materials or supplies necessary for construction or operation of the Vessel which the Builder or the Buyer may acquire① at its cost and by its own discretion② from abroad for the construction of the vessel.

The Builder shall bear the import duties, if any, imposed by Japan upon materials which will be acquired by the Builder from abroad for the construction of the vessel under the terms of this Contract.

(Excerpts from the contract of Nippon Kokan Kaboshiki Kaisha.)

Contract Effectiveness③, etc.

---

① 获得 ②判断力 ③有效期

1) This Contract is signed by the representatives of the Buyer and Seller in Beijing on 6 July, 19--. This Contract shall come into force[①] immediately after signature.

2) This Contract is made in both Chinese and English languages and there shall be two copies of each. The Buyer shall hold one copy each of Chinese and English and the Seller shall do likewise. Both versions[②] of the Contract are authentic[③].

3) All the correspondence[④], agreements and other documents in connection with the present Contract and made out by both parties prior to the signing of the present Contract shall be null and void after this Contract is signed.

4) Should any of the contents of this contract be amended and supplemented[⑤] by both parties, then documents in written form shall be signed by the representatives of both parties and such documents shall form as integral part of this Contract.

5) Appendix No. 1 to 8 of this Contract shall all form an intergral part of this Contract.

(Excerpts from the Contract between the MACHIMPEX and Jaybeng.)

Effectiveness of the present contract and miscellaneous[⑥].

1) The present Contract is signed between the authorized representatives of both parties on December lst, in Beijing and becomes effective immediately after the signing[⑦].

---

① 生效 ②版本 ③有效 ④信函 ⑤修改与补充⑥其它 ⑦签字后马上生效

2) The present Contract is made out in the English language in quadruplicate[①], the Buyer and Seller hold two copies each.

3) All the correspondence, agreements and other documents made out by both parties prior to the signature of the present contract will be null and void after signing the present contract.

4) Should any part of the present Contract be amended, documents in writing to be signed by authorized representatives of the Buyer and Seller shall be considered an integral part of the present Contract.

5) No assignment of any obligation[②] arising under this Contract shall be made by any of the parties to a third party without the previous consent of the other party.

6) Annex Nos. 1, 2, 3, 4, 5, 6, 7, 8, 9, and 10. . . shall be taken as an integral part of the present contract and The correspondance between twoparties during the execution of the present Contract shall all be made out in the English language, and all correspondence between the Buyer and the Seller shall be done in triplicate in English.

7) Neither party to the Contract shall be liable for consequential and/or indirect damages as a consequence of the fulfillment or nonfulfillment of their duties under the present Con-

① 一式四份 ②义务转让

tract.

8) The present Contract shall be null and void upon thedate of fulfillment of the duties by both parties under the present Contract.

(Excerpts from the contract for ammonia plant)

Miscellaneous

1) This Agreement is signed on the date first written above in duplicate original and shall be in full force and effect as from said date.

2) This agreement is written in the English language. Both parties shall hold one (1) of the duplicate originals of the agreement.

3) The captions[2] of the terms and conditions of this Agreement are for convenience of reference[3] only and shall not be construed as in any way limiting or extending the language of the provisions to which the captions refer.

4) Until further notice in writing from MACHIMPEX, any notice or information herein provided to be given by UACL to MACHIMPEEX shall be given by air mail, postage prepaid[4], addressed to the China National Machinery Import & Export Corp, P. O. Box 49, Beijing, the People's Republic of China, or, if sent by cable or radio[5] to the cable address, MACHIMPEX Beijing, the People's Republic of China. Until futher notice in writing from UACL, any notice or communica-

---

① 完全生效 ②标题 ③便于参考 ④邮费预付 ⑤电传或无线电传送

tion to be given by MACHIMPEX to UACL shall be given by airmail, postage prepaid, addressed to United Aircraft of Canada Limited, P. O. Box 10, Longueil, Quebec, Canada, or, if sent by cable or radio to the cable address "UNITEDAIR" Montreal Quebec, Canada.

5) No modification or amendment of this Agreement shall be binding unless in writing and signed by the respective parties hereto.

6) No interest in this agreement or the orders placed hereunder shall be assignable by either MACHIMPEX or UACL unless such assignment is mutually agreed to in writing by the parties hereto.

7) The terms and conditions of this agreement constitute the entire agreement between the parties hereto and shall supersede ① all previous communications, representations or agreements, either oral or written, between the parties hereto with respect to the subject matter hereof, and no agreement or understanding varying or extending the same, or modifications in the goods ordered hereunder, shall be binding upon either party hereto unless in writing, signed by a duly authorized officer of representative thereof.

8) This Agreement shall be and remain in force and effect②, for one (1) year from the date hereof, and will be auto-

---

① 取代 ②保持有效

matically renewed[1] from year to year thereafter. Either party may terminate[2] this Agreement at any time upon thirty (30) days written notice of its intent to do so; provided, however, that any orders subject to the terms hereof which are partially or totally unfulfilled on the date of said termination shall continue to be subject to all the terms and conditions hereof.

In WITNESS WHEREOF[3], the parties hereto have caused this Agreement to be executed in duplicate as of the day and year first above written.

(Excerpts from the Agreement between MACHIMPEX and UACL.)

---

① 续期(继续有效) ②使中止 ③为证明上述各节;为此:法律文件结束语

APPENDIX

CONTRACT

No. ______________

BEIJING. Date: __________

The Buyers: CHINA NATIONAL MACHINERY IMPORT AND EXPORT CORPORATION.

Address: Erligou, Xijiao, BEIJING, People' s Republic of China

Cable Address: "MACHIMPEX" BEIJING

TELEX: CMIEC CN

The Sellers: ______________________________

Address: ________________ TELEX: ______________

This Contract is made by and between the Buyers and the Sellers; whereby the Buyers agree to buy and the Sellers agree to sell the undermentioned commodity according to the terms and conditions stipulated below:

1.

ltem No.	Commodity,Specifications	Unit	Guan.	Unit Price	Total Amount
Total Value:					

2. COUNTRY OF ORIGIN AND MANUFACTURERS:

3. PACKING: To be packed in strong wooden case(s) or in carton (s), suitable for long distance ocean/parcel post/air freight transportation and to change of climate, well protected against moisture and shocks.

The Sellers shall be liable for any damage of the commodity and expenses incurred on account of improper packing and for any rust attributable to inadequate or improper protective measures taken by the Sellers in regard to the packing.

One full set of Service and operaton instructions concerned shall be enclosed in the case(s).

4. SHIPPING MARK: The Sellers shall mark in each package with fadeless paint the package number, gross weight, measurment and the wordings: " KEEP AWAY FROM

MOISTURE" "HANDLE WITH CARE","THIS SIDE UP" etc. and the shipping mark:

5. TIME OF SHIPMENT:

6. PORT OF SHIPMENT:

7. PORT OF DESTINATION:

8. INSURANCE: To be covered by the Buyers after shipment.

9. PAYMENT: Under (A) (B) (C) below:

(A) UNDER LETTER CREDIT: The Buyers, upon receipt from the Sellers of the delivery advice specified in Clause 11 (1) a hereof, shall, 15-20 days prior to the date of delivery, open an irrevocable letter of credit with Bank of China, Beijing, in favour of the Sellers for the total value of shipment. The credit shall be available against Sellers' draft (s) at sight on the opening bank for 100% invoice value accompanied by the shipping documents specified in Clause 10 hereof. Payment shall be effected by the opening bank, (by telegraphic transfer/airmail transfer) against presentation to them of the aforesaid draft (s) and documents. THE LETTER OF CREDIT shall be valid until the 15th day after the shipment is effected.

(B) ON COLLECTION: After shipment, the Sellers may draw on the Buyers at sight and send the draft(s) together with the shipping documents specified in Clause 10 hereof, to the Buyers through the Sellers' bankers and Bank of China, Beijing for collection.

(C) BY DIRECT REMITTANCE: Payment shall be effected by the Buyers, by telegraphic transfer/airmail transfer, within seven days after receipt from the Sellers of the shipping documents specified in Clause 10 hereof.

10. DOCUMENTS:

(1) In case of sea-freight

Full set of clean on board ocean Bills of Lading marked "Freight to Collect" made out to order blank endorsed notifying China National Foreign Trade Transportation Corporation at the port of destination.

In case of air-freight:

One copy of airway bill marked "Freight Prepaid" and consigned to the China National Foreign Trade Transportation Corporation at the airport of destination notifying the Buyers.

In case of air parcel post:

One copy of air parcel post receipt addressed to the Buyers.

(2) Invoice in 5 copies indicating contract number and

shipping mark (in case of more than one shipping mark the invoice shall be issued separately), made out in details as per the relative contract.

(3) Packing list in 2 copies issued by the Manufacturers.

(4) Certificate of Quality and Quantity issued by the Manufacturers.

(5) Copy of cable/telex to the buyers advising particulars of shipment immediately after shipment is made.

In addition, the sellers shall, within 10 days after shipment, send by airmail two extra sets of the aforesaid documents (except item 5), one set directly to the Buyers and one set directly to the China National Foreign Trade Transportation Corporation at the port of destinaton.

11. SHIPMENT:

(1) In case of FOB Terms:

a. The Sellers shall, 30 days before the date of shipment stipulated in the contract, advise the Buyers by cable/telex of the Contract No., commodity, quantity, value, number of package, gross weight, measurement and date of readiness at the port of shipment for the Buyers to book shipping space.

b. Booking of shipping space shall be attended to by the Buyers' Shipping Agents Messrs. China National Chartering Corporation, Beijing, China (Cable address:

Sinochart Beijing).

c. China National Chartering Corporation, Beijing, China, or it's Port Agents (or Liners' Agents), shall send to the Sellers 10 days before the estimated date of arrival of the vessel at the port of shipment, a preliminary notice indicating the name of vessel, estimated date of loadng, Contract No. for the Sellers to arrange shipment. The Sellers are requested to get in close contact with the shipping agents. When it becomes necessary to change the carrying vessel or in the event of her arrival having to be advanced or delayed, the Buyers or the Shipping Agent shall advise the Sellers in time. Should the vessel fail to arrive at the port of loading within 30 days after the arrival date advised by the Buyers, the Buyers shall bear the storage and insurance expenses incurred from the 31st day.

d. The Sellers shall be liable for any dead freight or demurrage, should it happen that they have failed to have the commodity ready for loading after the carrying vessel has arrived at the port of shipment on time.

e. The Sellers shall bear all expenses, risks of the commodity before it passes over the vessel's rail and is released from the tackle. After it has passed over the vessel's rail and been released from the tackle, all expenses of the commodity shall be for the Buyers' account.

(2) In case of CFR Terms:

a. The Sellers shall ship the goods within the shipment time from the port of shipment to the port of destination. Transshipment is not allowed. The contracted goods shall not be carried by a vessel flying the flag of the country which the Buyers can not accept. The age of vessel should not exceed 15 years.

b. In case the goods are to be despatched by parcel post/air-freight, the Sellers shall, 30 days before the time of delivery as stipulated in Clause 5, inform the Buyers by cable/telex of the estimated date of delivery, Contract No, commodity, invoiced value, etc. The Sellers shall, immediately after despatch of the goods, advise the Buyers by cable/telex of the Contract No. , commodity, invoiced value and date of despatch for the Buyers to arrange insurance in time.

12. SHIPPING ADVICE:

a. In case of FOB terms:

The Sellers shall, immediately upon the completion of the loading of the goods, advise by cable/telex the Buyers of the Contract No. , commodity, quantity, invoiced value, gross weight, name of vessel and date of sailing etc. In case the Buyers fail to arrange insurance in time due to the Sellers not having cabled in time all losses shall be borne by the Sellers.

b. In case of CFR terms:

The Sellers shall, immediately upon the completion of the loading of the goods, advise by cable/telex the buyers of the Contract No. commodity, quantity, invoiced value, gross weight, name of vessel, length, draft, lifting capacity of the vessel and date of sailing, etc.

13. GUARANTEE OF QUALITY:

The Sellers guarantee that the Commodity hereof is made of the best material with first class workmanship, brand new and unused, and complies in all respects with the quality and specification stipulated in this Contract. The guarantee period shall be 12 months counting from the date on which the commodity arrives at the port of destination.

14. CLAIMS:

Within 90 days after the arrival of the goods at destination, should the quality, specification, or quantity be found not in conformity with the stipulations of the Contract except those claims for which the insurance company or the owners of the vessel are liable, the Buyers shall, on the strength of the Inspection Certificate issued by the China Commodity Inspection Bureau, have the right to claim for replacement with new goods, or for compensation, and all the expenses (such as inspection charges, freight for returning the goods and for sending the replacement, insurance premium, storage and loading and unloading charges etc.) shall be borne by the Sellers. As regards quality, the Sellers shall guarantee that if within 12 months from the date of arrival of the goods at destination, damages occur in the course of operation by reason of inferior quality, bad workmanship or the use of inferior materials, the Buyers shall immediately notify the Sellers in writing and put forward a claim supported by Inspection Certificate issued by the China Import and Export Commodity Inspection Bureau.

The Certificate so issued shall be accepted as the base of a claim. The Sellers, in accordance with the Buyers' claim, shall be responsible for the immediate elimination of the defect (s), complete or partial replacement of the commodity or shall devaluate the commodity according to the state of defect(s). Where necessary, the Buyers shall be at liberty to eliminate the defect(s) themselves at the Sellers' expenses. If the Sellers fail to answer the Buyers within one month after receipt of the aforesaid claim, the claim shall be reckoned as having been accepted by the Sellers.

15. FORCE MAJEURE:

The Sellers shall not be held responsible for the delay in shipment or non-delivery of the goods due to Force Majeure, which might occur during the process of manufacturing or in the course of loading or transit. The Sellers shall advise the Buyers immediately of the occurrence mentioned above and within fourteen days thereafter, the Sellers shall send by airmail to the Buyers for their acceptance a certificate of the acccident issued by the Competent Government Authorities where the accident occurs as evidence thereof. Under such circumstances the Sellers, however, are still under the obligation to take all necessary measures to hasten the delivery of the goods. In case the accident lasts for more than 10 weeks, the Buyers shall have the right to cancel the Contract.

16. LATE DELIVERY AND PENALTY:

Should the Sellers fail to make delivery on time as stipulated in the Contract, with exception of Force Majeure causes specified in Clause 15 of this Contract, the Buyers shall agree to postpone the delivery on condition that the Sellers agree to pay a penalty which shall be deducted by the paying bank from the payment. The penalty, however, shall not exceed 5% of the total value of the goods involved in the late delivery. The rate of penalty is charged at 0.5% for every seven days, odd days less than seven days should be counted as seven days. In case the Sellers fail to make delivery ten weeks later than the time of shipment stipulated in the Contract, the Buyers shall have the right to cancel the Contract and the Sellers, in spite of the cancellation, shall still pay the aforesaid penalty to the Buyers without delay.

17. ARBITRATION:

All disputes in connection with this Contract or the execution thereof shall be settled friendly through negotiations. In case no settlement can be reached, the case may then be submitted for arbitration to the Arbitration Commission of the China Council for the Promotion of International Trade in accordance with the Provisional Rules of Procedures promulgated by the said Arbitration Commission. The Arbitration shall take place in Beijing and the decision of the Arbitration Committee shall be final and binding upon both parties; neither party shall seek recourse to a law court nor other authorities to appeal for revision of the decision. Arbitration fee shall be borne by the losing party. Or the Arbitration may be settled in the third country mutually agreed upon by both parties.

18. SPECLAL PROVISIONS:

IN WITNESS THEREOF, this contract is signed by both parties in two original copies; each party holds one copy.

THE BUYERS: THE SELLERS:

CHINA NATIONAL MACHINERY IMPORT AND EXPORT CORPORATION

(京)新登字 182 号

图书在版编目(CIP)数据

国际销售合同/诸葛霖等编著. 一北京:对外贸易教育出版社,1994

ISBN 7-81000-690-8

Ⅰ.国… Ⅱ.诸… Ⅲ.国际贸易-贸易合同-基本知识 Ⅳ.F740.4

中国版本图书馆 CIP 数据核字(94)第 08939 号

对外贸易教育出版社出版

社址:北京惠新东街 12 号　　邮政编码:100029

建设部政策研究中心科建照排部排版

经贸大学印刷厂印刷　　新华书店北京发行所发行

787×1092　1/32　8.5 印张　191 千字

1994 年 8 月北京第 1 版　1994 年 8 月北京第 1 次印刷

ISBN 7-81000-690-8/H·144　　责任编辑:王敬之

印数 0001—5000 册　　定价:9.00 元